Monsters
of the Deep

Monsters
of the Deep

Sharks, Giant Squid, Whales and Dolphins

Heather Angel

LONGMEADOW
PRESS

First published in the USA by
Longmeadow Press, PO Box 16,
Rowayton Station, Norwalk,
Connecticut 06853

© 1976 Octopus Books Limited

ISBN 0 7064 0541 2

Produced by Mandarin Publishers Limited
22A Westlands Road, Quarry Bay, Hong Kong

Printed by Jarrold & Sons Limited

Contents

Great White and other Sharks

The most infamous of all 'monsters' of the deep is undoubtedly the shark, and more than any other known animal, it arouses universal respect, excitement and fear in man. Stories of encounters between the two that stretch back to prehistoric times, prove the antipathy has existed for centuries, although even today very little is known about their life style and behavioural patterns. Everybody, however, is alive to their potential danger — swimmers, water-skiers, skin divers and yachtsmen who frequent shark infested waters, particularly so. Over the years, the word 'shark' has come to be synonymous with teeth, so that any shark, regardless of its species, is automatically considered harmful, while the unmistakeable torpedo-shape and evil looking, erect fins, are likely to incite fear in all who sight them. With the publicity that has been given to the gruesome results of shark attacks, it is hardly surprising that an authentic model placed in an appropriate location would evoke much the same response of fear and frenzy as a live specimen would do.

The amazing fact however, is that the majority of sharks are harmless to man. Out of the 300 or so known species, only twenty seven are on record as making unprovoked attacks on men or boats and statistics prove indisputably, that the likelihood of being attacked by a shark is extremely remote.

One of the few predictable facts about sharks is that they are extremely unpredictable, as illustrated by the US Navy Manual which says: "All you have to do is look at the record. Never count on a shark not attacking you. He may do it."

The sharks that frequent our waters today are a primitive group of vertebrate animals, closely related to species, which existed as far back as the Jurassic Period of 140-170 million years ago. Unlike the bony fishes, the skeletons of sharks are composed of cartilage, and as this does not fossilize so readily as bone, fossil sharks, as such, are a comparative rarity. However, the hard enamel coating on shark teeth has ensured abundant fossil records of this part of their anatomy—the huge teeth of the giant fossil shark *Carcharodon megalodon*, being a famous example. The 10cm (4in) long teeth indicate that this shark may have reached a length of 20m (60ft) or more and the American Museum of Natural History have a photograph showing six men standing inside a model reconstruction of its jaws.

Cartilaginous and bony fishes both have jaws, and are therefore classified together with amphibians, birds and mammals, in the major vertebrate group known as Gnathostomata. The jawless lampreys and hagfishes are classified in the other major group—the Agnatha.

Almost the only feature which sharks share with true bony fishes, is that they both live in an aquatic environment, but it is here that the similarity ends! They have extensive differences in both anatomical features and physiological processes, such as their type of skeleton, their salt and water balance and their method of reproduction. In addition sharks have exposed gill slits with no gill covering and like the rays, are covered with backwardly-pointing, tooth-like placoid scales (the 'shark skin') which contrast to the rounded scales of the bony fishes.

The origin or derivation of the word shark is not certain although usage in popular language is clear enough. A loosely defined distinction is made between the large and the small sharks; large species are always referred to as 'sharks', while smaller species are known as 'dogfish' or 'huss', although they are essentially small sharks. In fact the dogfish is frequently used as one of the type specimens for zoology and medical students. The rays (discussed in the next chapter) constitute yet another group and can be termed 'flattened' sharks.

Sharks are sometimes collectively referred to by the colloquial names of elasmobranchs, selachians or squalids. Elasmobranchii form one of the three major divisions of jawed fish, to which the chimaeras (ratfish), sharks and rays belong, and to which fossil shark-like fishes such as *Climatius* and *Coccosteus* used to belong. Selachii is the name used by some people for the modern sharks and rays, and by others for all cartilaginous fishes, including fossil forms and chimaeras. *Squalus* is the latin word for shark, although the family Squalidae comprises the spiny dogfishes and not the larger fearsome sharks. The French word for shark is *requin* and the German *Haifisch*, while the British Navy has coined its own word for sharks, dubbing them nobbies.

There are rather gruesome accounts of what happens when sailors catch a shark at sea; they

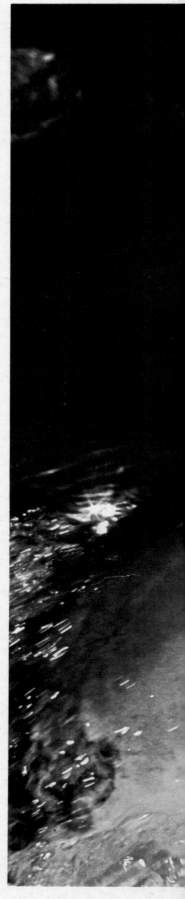

immediately set about killing it as quickly as possible. It is as if the sight of a shark turns the men berserk, and their instinctive actions develop into a primitive blood bath orgy.

As sharks have long fired man's imagination, known facts about them have inevitably become entangled with myths and legends. In recent years, the upsurge of skin-diving, coupled with 'shark' books, and films, has aroused world-wide interest and in many cases, even among arm-chair addicts who are unlikely to visit tropical waters, this has developed into an insatiable curiosity. And yet from a zoological standpoint, there is still so much to be discovered about the habits, the behaviour, the life history and the longevity of sharks.

How long sharks live is one aspect that is particularly uncertain. They are known to be afflicted by few, if any, diseases, so in most cases, unless caught by man, they die of 'old age'. Quite what this constitutes in a shark is almost pure speculation. It is known however, that sharks have a remarkable tenacity for life. There is a story of a shark which, after being caught, had been gutted, and thrown back into the sea, only to be hooked with its own intestines used as bait! Similar stories tell of sharks seen attempting to swim when tossed overboard with their jaws removed for souvenirs, and their gonads and guts opened out.

Apart from other sharks and man, not surprisingly sharks have few enemies. Dolphins have been known to attack sharks in aquaria, as was illustrated in America when a female dolphin was about to give birth. Other vigilant dolphins took it in turns to ram their snouts against the abdomen of a shark, and although no external wounds were produced, the shark died within minutes, from a ruptured gut. It is doubtful, however, that such an attack would take place in the open sea. Salt water

crocodiles will also attack sharks and the small porcupine fish can asphyxiate a shark by inflating itself inside its attacker's mouth, thus preventing water passing out through the gills.

There are between 250 and 350 species of shark. The fact that each year new species are discovered, while others are demoted from a species in their own right to being variants of others, makes it impossible to be more precise. Taken collectively, they span a huge size range and have amongst their number, the largest fish in the world. This is the Whale Shark *Rhincodon typus* (often misspelt *Rhineodon* or *Rhinodon*), found in the warmer areas of the Atlantic, Pacific and Indian oceans and which can reach 19 m (59 ft) long. Like the 15 m (45 ft) long Basking Shark, *Cetorhinus maximus*, the Whale Shark is not a man-eater, and both species feed solely on plankton. The smallest known species of shark is the Midwater Shark *Squaliolus laticaudus*, which becomes mature at 15 cm (6 in) long.

Not all sharks inhabit tropical or near tropical seas; some live in temperate waters and some are even found in Arctic waters. Indeed not all sharks live in the sea; some inhabit rivers and lakes—the renowned man-eating sharks of Lake Nicaragua for example. Some marine sharks live close to the surface, while others prefer the darker depths of the ocean. In general sharks are drably coloured, usually having a darker back and a lighter belly. The common name of some sharks, such as the Zebra Shark, indicates the colouration of the upper dorsal surface. Other colourful species, are the Carpet Sharks and Wobbegongs.

It is always unwise to think in terms of a 'typical' animal, since through the process of evolution, differences—some small, some great—have come to exist between species within a group. In spite of

this, and the great variation in size and type of habitat in which sharks occur, there are basic features which are recognizable in most species, (see page 11). A shark's front end is usually pointed, projecting beyond its underslung mouth and on each side of its body, behind its eyes, there are usually five (sometimes six or seven), open gill slits. Behind each row of slits is a swept-back pectoral fin, which unlike the flexible and often highly mobile pectorals of bony fishes, are rigid and cannot be used as brakes. Instead these paired fins, which are larger than the more posterior paired pelvic fins, are used like the wings of an aircraft, to provide lift. A shark's tail or caudal fin is asymmetrical, with a larger upper lobe, and when this so-called heterocercal tail beats, it gives a lifting force to the tail end. This would tilt the shark's head downwards if it was not balanced by the angle of the pectorals tending to plane the head

LEFT A Sand Shark (*Odontaspis taurus*) with its mouth open taking in water while its gill slits are closed. It then closes its mouth and the water is pumped over its gills and out of the slits.

FAR RIGHT The Zambezi Shark (*Carcharhinus zambezensis*) has been described as 'a particularly ferocious species which will attack large fish without apparent provocation and not for food.'

RIGHT A large Black-Tipped Shark (*Carcharhinus* sp.) shows many characteristic shark features: the streamlined torpedo shape and the relationship of the mouth, eyes and gill slits.

BELOW RIGHT Beneath a coral head on the Great Barrier reef lies a Tasselled Wobbegong Shark (*Orectolobus ogilbyi*), while over it, hover shoals of tiny fish that form its basic diet.

BELOW The mouths of most sharks are underslung on their head. Their eyes are mounted on the sides of the head, limiting both their field of forward vision and their ability to see what they are biting.

BELOW RIGHT A Sand Shark (*Ginglymostoma brevicaudatum*) swims overhead, showing how the top lobe of its tail is greatly elongated. Beating this lobe gives both forward propulsive force and lift to the tail end.

upwards, thereby keeping it on an even keel when swimming. This lift also serves to keep the shark up in the water, necessary because they have no swim-bladder and their specific gravity is greater than that of sea water. If they were to stop swimming, they would immediately begin to sink. The perpetual swimming motion not only prevents a shark from sinking, it also provides a continuous supply of oxygenated water over the gills. As water enters a shark's mouth the gill slits are closed so that water cannot enter through them. The shark then closes its mouth and the water passes to the gill region. Finally, the gill slits open and the water passes out through them. Divers can revive a motionless shark by pulling or pushing it through the water, forcing it to swim. Conversely, a shark can be subdued by pulling it backwards through water, a technique which film directors have used.

For most of the time, sharks maintain an even speed, but since they are capable of sudden bursts of energy, they are referred to as 'sprinters', in contrast to whales which are termed the 'stayers'. Sharks have two types of swimming muscles, one red and the other white. The red muscle is coloured by its rich content of myoglobin, which is a respiratory pigment similar to the haemoglobin in our blood. It also acts as an oxygen store. The

blood supply to the red muscle has a counterflow system, so that the incoming arterial blood flows adjacent to the outgoing venous blood. This acts as a heat exchange system, with the effect of warming up the red muscle, so it works more powerfully and efficiently than the white muscle. The white muscle is used for short bursts of speed and it gets its energy from breaking down stored glycogen into lactic acid in an anaerobic process. The red muscle, on the other hand, gains its energy by breaking down glycogen by oxidation.

The two fastest moving sharks, the Porbeagle (*Lamna nasus*) and the Mako (*Isurus oxyrinchus*) both have a body temperature above sea water, which increases the extent of the muscular contractions. In short bursts, a Great Blue Shark (*Prionace glauca*) is capable of reaching a speed of 69 km/h (43 mph). The 50 km/h (31 mph) speed of the Mako Shark may seem at first to be less impressive, but it can be sustained over a distance of 0.8 km (0.5 mile).

The ability of sharks to scent their quarry is legendary; so much so, they have been described as a 'swimming nose'. Most sharks have nostrils opening on the underside of their heads—exceptions being the Hammerheads and the Whale Shark where they occur on the leading edge of the head.

The enlarged fore lobes, which constitute about two-thirds of a shark's brain, are concerned with the sense of smell or the olfactory sense. The scent detectors are sensory cells situated inside paired olfactory sacs leading from the nostrils. The importance and efficiency of these sensory cells was shown from experiments conducted by American scientists in the early part of this century. Freshly killed and punctured crabs were introduced into an aquarium with a smooth dogfish (*Mustelus canis*), which straight away homed in on the crabs by swimming in tighter and tighter circles. The crabs were then wrapped up in cloth, but still the dogfish could find them, and it was also shown to be able to distinguish between covered crabs and covered stones. When its nostrils were plugged however, the dogfish was unable to locate the crabs at all.

Sharks can detect variations in strength of an odour by moving their head from side to side as they swim. In this way, they 'taste' the water in a wide arc so they are able to home in towards the direction of the most powerful odour.

In addition to the well-developed olfactory sense, sharks have three other kinds of sense organs, namely the lateral line sensory canals, the Ampullae of Lorenzini and sensory pits. All fish have lateral lines and in sharks, the canals are filled with mucus, which explains why they are sometimes known as 'mucus canals'. They are particularly sensitive to low frequency vibrations. The openings to the Ampullae of Lorenzini are marked by small pores on the head of sharks. Various functions of these organs have been proposed, such as the ability to react to temperature, salinity and pressure, but it seems they can also detect electrical impulses given off by potential prey. If this is so, they would be particularly useful to bottom-living, or benthic, species. Sensory pits occur all over the body of sharks, but they are more numerous in open water species, than in the benthic types. At the base of each pit are sense organs, which it is thought may function in the same way as our own taste buds.

The acuity of shark vision is debatable. The retina in each eye contains many rod cells which are sensitive to monochrome vision in low levels of light intensity but until recently the presence of colour-sensitive cone cells had not been detected. However, these have now been found in the retinas of at least fifteen shark species, and perhaps means they could be attracted to brightly coloured swim suits!

The eyes of mammals can be focused on near or distant objects by a change in the internal lens curvature. In bony fishes and lampreys, the eyes are normally focused on close objects, and the lenses are moved backwards to bring distant objects into focus. Sharks eyes, on the other hand, are generally focused for distant viewing, and the lenses are moved forward to perceive close-ups. The visual sensitivity of sharks in poor lighting is increased by a silvery reflective layer beneath the retina, known as the tapetum lucidum. This comprises a layer of plates which reflect light as it passes through the retina, and it also makes the eyes glow when any light is shone on to them. In brightly lit locations, sharks have two devices for cutting down the amount of light passing through the eye. They can reduce the size of the pupil aperture and they can prevent reflection from the silvery tapetum, by spreading out black pigment granules between the plates.

It is the sense of smell however, that is probably a shark's dominant long-range tracking mechanism, although at close quarters it would seem that the sense of vision becomes increasingly important. The other main sense—that of hearing—still presents something of an enigma. It has been proved that some sharks are able to hear, particularly low-frequency sounds, but much more research needs to be done if this aspect of shark behaviour is to be understood further.

It is popularly believed that sharks are huge eaters. This is not true, and they certainly cannot, as is often quoted, eat the equivalent of their own body weight once a day. They would be better described as opportunist feeders, eating as and when they find food. When supplies are short, they are able to fast for quite long periods. The non-plankton eating species are both carnivores and scavengers, and sometimes even cannabalistic, especially if another has become entangled in a net. Sharks kept in captivity, provided with a constant supply of food, have been found to eat only ten per cent or even less, of their body weight during the course of a whole week.

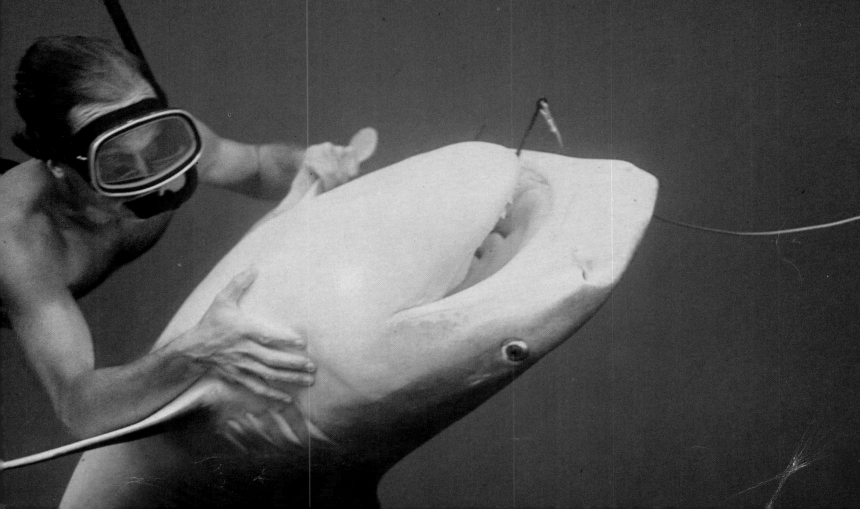

RIGHT As a Great White Shark (*Carcharodon carcharias*) gapes, its lower jaw swings forward and its eyes gaze fully to the front.

CENTRE A 2½ m (8ft) Australian Grey Nurse Shark (*Odontaspis arenarius*) makes a meal of a 7kg (15lb) blue grouper.

FAR RIGHT The serrated teeth of a Great White Shark (*Carcharodon carcharias*) portray its carnivorous habit.

BELOW RIGHT The Port Jackson Shark (*Heterodontus philippi*) have two types of teeth— cutting incisors and grinding molars.

Another myth that needs exploding is that because they have an underslung mouth, sharks must always turn on their sides to feed. Observations made of sharks feeding both in the open sea and in aquaria show they are perfectly adept at feeding on fishes swimming on a level or below them, without rolling their bodies. It is true though, that sharks can and do roll to feed on a baited hook or on a floating object, so perhaps it is reasonable that observers in boats would tend to assume this to be the normal rather than exceptional, method of attack. Some species, such as the Great White Shark thrust their lower jaw-bone forward as they open their mouth, so making the gape both larger and more awesome.

The feature which one most instantly thinks of at the merest mention of sharks—those infamous teeth—are an important aid to shark identification. In fact teeth marks alone left behind in the subject of an attack by each genus of the family *Isuridae* (which includes the Great White Shark), are sufficient to identify the particular species. The cutting teeth of these sharks are typically triangular in shape, and they have either a smooth or serrated edge.

The jaw teeth of sharks are like large scale versions of the outer skin teeth and in most species, they consist of those notorious sharp-pointed teeth used for seizing and biting the prey. The Port Jackson Shark *Herterodontus*, however, has two types of teeth; incisors at the front of the jaw which it uses for cutting and then, behind these, there are some crushing molars.

Shark teeth are not embedded in sockets like those of man, nor is it uncommon for a shark to lose several teeth during its lifetime. But this does not mean they continue life as toothless wonders, for behind the row of functional teeth lie several replacement rows which can be used when the front teeth are lost. The Lemon Shark (*Negaprion brevirostris*) for example, can replace lost teeth in just over a week.

Although sharks have distinct food preferences, which will be described later as individual species are considered, some very curious objects have been found inside the stomachs of sharks. Leaving aside the gruesome discoveries of parts of the human anatomy, some of the more bizarre objects are listed by Lineaweaver and Backus in their book 'The Natural History of Sharks'. A raincoat, three overcoats and a car licence plate were found inside a shark caught in the Adriatic. While an Australian shark was found to have consumed a goat, a turtle, a large tomcat, three birds, four fish heads and a 2m (6ft) long shark. Inside the stomachs of other sharks caught at other times and places were found six hens and a rooster; twenty five bottles of Vichy Water bound together with a wire hoop; a nearly whole reindeer; a ship's scraper; six horseshoe crabs; three bottles of beer; a blue penguin; a piece of bark from an oak tree; parts of porpoises; a 45kg (100lb) loggerhead turtle; a handbag containing three shillings, a powderpuff and a wristwatch; sting rays; a full grown spaniel; seaweed; a Galapagos seal pup; orange peel; squids; an 11kg (25lb) lump of whale blubber and seven strands of whalebone; paper cups; and a yellow-billed cuckoo." The only possible conclusion one can draw from this list is that sharks are far from selective about their intake! Instead they are rather like a vacuum cleaner, and will ingest virtually anything which happens to be in their way—further proof that they are opportunist feeders.

Leading from a shark's U-shaped stomach, is the gut or intestine, the internal spiral valve of which effectively increases the surface area of the gut for absorption. This primitive feature provides an alternative solution to an increase in the length of the gut itself, and is not unique to sharks. It is also known to occur in the sturgeons, bichirs, lungfishes and bowfins.

All shark eggs, including those of rays and dogfish, are fertilized internally. The hind part of the male's pelvic fins is modified into claspers, and these play an important part during the process of

BELOW RIGHT The
Common Sand Shark of
South African waters, is
known as the Ragged
Toothed Shark (*Odontaspis
taurus*). It can inflict terrible
injuries on its victims.

RIGHT Inspecting one of
the meshing nets set to
keep an Australian beach
safe, a diver finds a live
Great White Shark
(*Carcharodon carcharias*)
entangled in it.

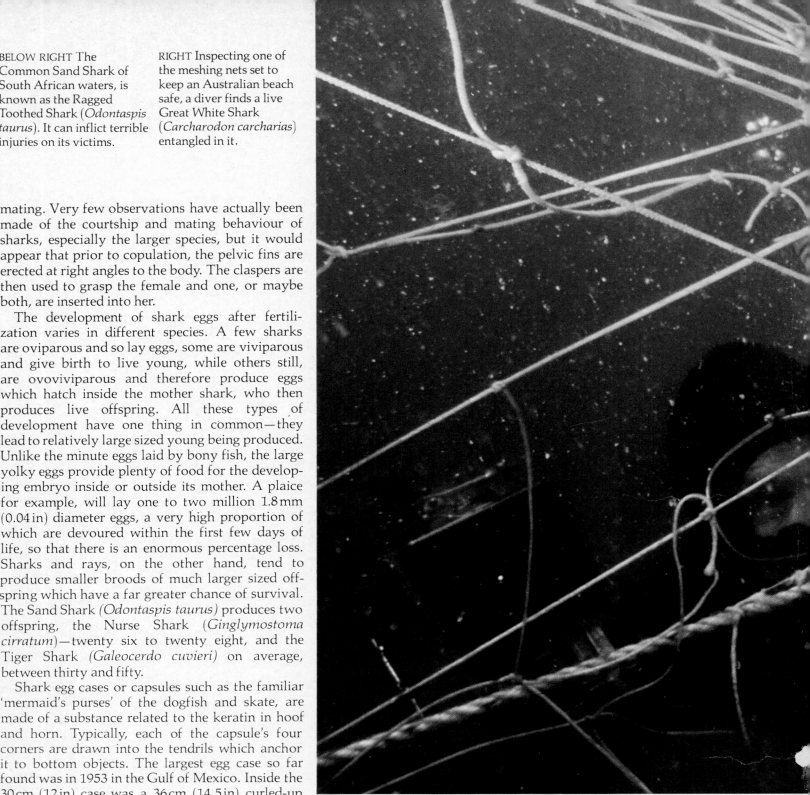

mating. Very few observations have actually been made of the courtship and mating behaviour of sharks, especially the larger species, but it would appear that prior to copulation, the pelvic fins are erected at right angles to the body. The claspers are then used to grasp the female and one, or maybe both, are inserted into her.

The development of shark eggs after fertilization varies in different species. A few sharks are oviparous and so lay eggs, some are viviparous and give birth to live young, while others still, are ovoviviparous and therefore produce eggs which hatch inside the mother shark, who then produces live offspring. All these types of development have one thing in common—they lead to relatively large sized young being produced. Unlike the minute eggs laid by bony fish, the large yolky eggs provide plenty of food for the developing embryo inside or outside its mother. A plaice for example, will lay one to two million 1.8mm (0.04in) diameter eggs, a very high proportion of which are devoured within the first few days of life, so that there is an enormous percentage loss. Sharks and rays, on the other hand, tend to produce smaller broods of much larger sized offspring which have a far greater chance of survival. The Sand Shark *(Odontaspis taurus)* produces two offspring, the Nurse Shark (*Ginglymostoma cirratum*)—twenty six to twenty eight, and the Tiger Shark *(Galeocerdo cuvieri)* on average, between thirty and fifty.

Shark egg cases or capsules such as the familiar 'mermaid's purses' of the dogfish and skate, are made of a substance related to the keratin in hoof and horn. Typically, each of the capsule's four corners are drawn into the tendrils which anchor it to bottom objects. The largest egg case so far found was in 1953 in the Gulf of Mexico. Inside the 30cm (12in) case was a 36cm (14.5in) curled-up embryonic Whale Shark—a miniature replica of the adult.

Sharks are usually either viviparous or ovoviviparous, and the gestation periods may be as long as two years, which is amongst the longest of any vertebrate animal. In ovoviviparous species the fertilized egg becomes enclosed in a very thin membrane, which is soon shed so that the embryo grows inside the female uterus. It feeds on its own yolk sac, until it is born, although in some species, once they have absorbed the yolk, the embryos will begin to feed on unfertilized eggs which enter the uterus. This egg feeding, or oophagy, is known to occur in the Porbeagle and the Mako Shark. The viviparous sharks also develop their young internally but a closer association is formed by the mother with the embryo. After the embryo passes to the uterus, an 'umbilical cord' forms with a 'yolk placenta' at the end. This placenta, although

not identical in structure to the mammalian placenta, none the less has the same function, allowing embryos to take nutrition from their mother as well as from the yolk sac. The discovery of young sharks inside adults once led to the belief that they must be mammals and not fish.

Of all the man-eating sharks, the Great White Shark (*Carcharodon carcharias*), is the most famous and the most feared by man. Also known as White Shark, White Death, Man-eater, White Pointer (Australia) and Blue Pointer (South Africa), it is the largest carnivorous fish in the world, although compared with the plankton-feeding Whale Shark, the maximum size of 11.28 m (37ft) so far recorded may seem unspectacular. This record sized White Shark was trapped in a herring weir at White Head Island, New Brunswick, Canada in 1930. When its weight (estimated to be 10,885 kg (24,000lb) is considered together with the notoriously well equipped, serrated-toothed jaws, even an average sized 5 m (15ft) long White Shark, weighing a mere 520-760 kg (1,150-1,700lb), is a fearsome enough carnivore for a diver or a swimmer to confront.

Dull slaty-blue or a greyish colour above and dirty white below, the White Shark is a pelagic, or oceanic species found in both tropical and temperate waters all over the world. It is easily the most aggressive of the man-eaters and always very much a 'lone-wolf'. An exceptional and extremely unusual incident involving a White Shark, is related by Captain Cousteau in his book *'The Silent World'* (1953):

"During an encounter with a shark in the Cape Verde Islands, at a distance of 40 feet there appeared from the grey haze the lead-white bulk

of a 25-foot *Carcharodon carcharias*, the only shark species that all specialists agree is a confirmed man-eater. Dumas, my bodyguard, closed in beside me. The brute was swimming lazily. Then the shark saw us. His reaction was the least conceivable one. In pure fright, the monster voided a cloud of excrement and departed at an incredible speed."

A cowardly reaction indeed! But one that proves again how impossible it is to predict how a shark will behave.

The White Shark has been held responsible for more attacks on men and boats than any other species, although it is not always easy to prove that a 'certain' identification is indisputably correct. Although bathers are at risk when White Sharks move close inshore, opportunities for attacking people are comparatively rare. White Sharks, or indeed any man-eaters, merely supplement their diet with an occasional human meal—a fact which must offer small compensation to the victim!

What is it that motivates a shark attack? To satisfy hunger would seem the most obvious reason; but this cannot explain all the attacks on boats or why sharks with full stomachs have often been caught on lines. Many boat attacks can be attributed to either a trail of fish guts thrown overboard or to similar seepage from leaky fishing boats. Likewise, fish damaged by spear fishermen will attract sharks and the diver's habit of threading speared fish onto a wire loop attached to the diver's belt, is the most frequent cause of shark injuries to skin divers. It is well known that blood attracts and excites sharks and they can detect human blood diluted by one part to between ten and a hundred million parts of sea water. In addition, vomit, waste food and putrefying flesh are all known to be shark attractants.

Disturbance of the surface water, by boat propellers or by overarm swimming, is often said to provoke shark attacks. This was convincingly bourne out on 25 July, 1936, at Buzzards Bay, Massachusetts, when one of two swimmers was singled out for attack by a White Shark. One was swimming side stroke and the other—the crawl, and it was the crawl swimmer who had his left leg bitten and who died after it had been amputated. Also, Dr. Conrad Limbaugh, who disappeared in 1960 whilst diving, said that splashing water attracted more sharks into an area. But before any definite conclusions are drawn from this, it would be as well to consider an account by Alain Gerbault, who relates how he managed to frighten off a shark by vigorous overarm swimming! Inexplicable unprovoked attacks are perhaps triggered by an aggressive impulse on the part of the shark, but really there seems to be no set pattern of events which lead to an attack. Cousteau, who has experienced over a hundred encounters with sharks, also emphasizes their totally unpredictable nature.

The fact that few successful attacks are observed in detail by onlookers is another reason why it is hard to reach conclusions about them. It is chiefly from the victims who have survived, that the fullest accounts of attacks are obtained, yet a victim is often unaware the first time he has been bitten, even extensively, by a shark. Frequently, accounts tell of a disturbance in the water or a nudging sensation, but not often a feeling of searing pain. The panic and fear set in only if the shark is sighted before the attack or when the sea around becomes discoloured with blood.

The idea of a solitary shark—a rogue shark—developing a taste for human flesh was first introduced by the Australian surgeon, Dr. Coppleson, who compared them with the man-eating lions and tigers. There have, however, been many accounts of so-called rogue sharks making multiple attacks

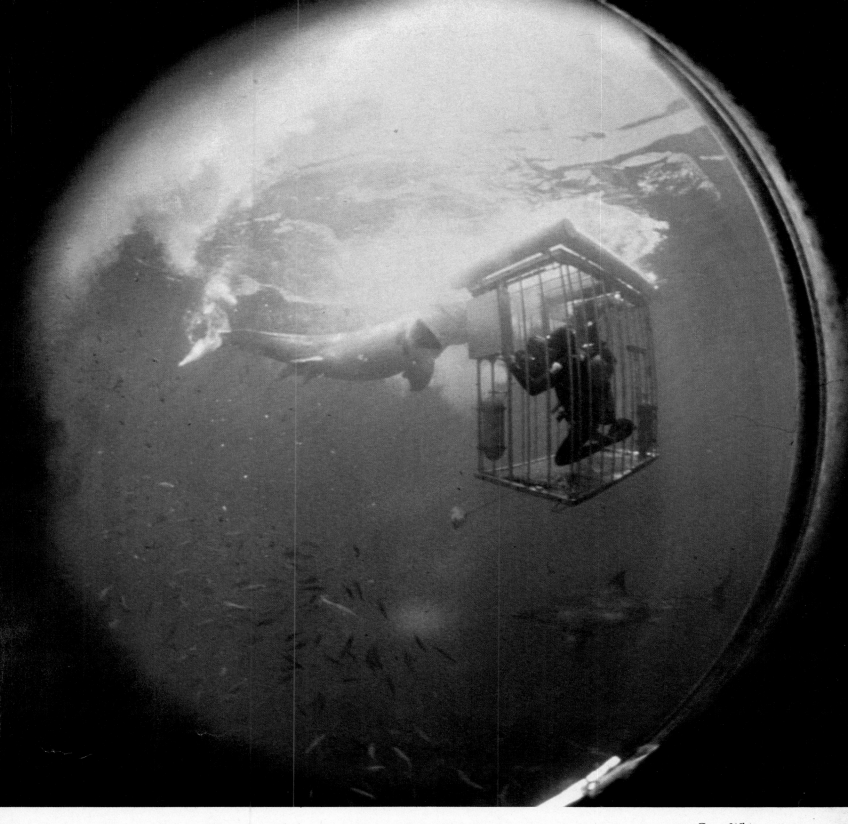

along the same stretch of coastline. One of these dates as far back as 1899, when at 8.30 am on August 8th, a thirteen year-old Arab boy, who had been bitten by a shark, was admitted to a hospital in Port Said. Another boy was brought in at 9.30 am and a third at 11.30 am. One explanation for these rogue sharks (known as *bank loafers* by Florida fishermen), suggested by Stewart Springer working in the Florida-Caribbean area, is that each migratory species in the temperate and sub-tropical Western North Atlantic has two distinct groups. There is the main breeding population, or *principal* population, and a dis-orientated *accessory* population, which gets out of tune with the reproductive cycle. It is from the latter group, the accessory population, that Springer thinks the rogue sharks emanate.

The temperature of the water appears to play an important part in shark attacks and the critical temperature seems to be 20-21°C (68-70°F). In equatorial regions, where the sea temperature remains above 23°C (74°F) (roughly between 21°N and 21°S), attacks may occur during any month of the year. In higher latitudes, attacks most often take place during the summer months; from May to October between 21 and 42°N, and from November to April between 21 and 42°S, which also correlates with the times of year most people go swimming in these latitudes. Unfortunately however, shark attacks are not completely confined to these parameters and there are recorded cases of attacks in the Mediterranean, including Genoa (44°24'N) and in waters off California, where temperatures were as low as 12°C (55°F).

ABOVE Great White Sharks (*Carcharodon carcharias*) are notorious for the violence of their unprovoked attacks. Here, one attracted by the blood in the water, turns its fury on the diver in a shark cage.

It has now been agreed that certain years can be classed as 'shark years', during which an above average number of attacks take place in a given area. 1916 was one such year in New Jersey when five attacks took place in twelve days, where none had occurred previously. Also in this year, Edwin Thorne, whose hobby was shark-catching, saw 277 sharks and killed 102, and yet during a seventeen year period, he neither saw nor killed as many in any other single year. 1961 turned out to be another 'shark year', this time in Australia where large numbers of sharks were sighted and at least fifteen Grey Nurse and White Pointers were killed. In addition two fatal attacks were made on humans in December off the Queensland coast. The explanation for this particular upsurge of sharks, lay in the heavy flooding which had swept many fish down rivers into the sea.

Typical of the general myths which surround sharks, it is in fact only comparatively recently, that the possibility of that greatest of horrors—the Great White—attacking man anywhere outside the tropics has become accepted. It was, after all, considered to be a tropical pelagic shark. As late as 1950, the California Bureau of Marine Fisheries published a guide to the sharks found in Californian Waters, in which it stated that the Great White was "uncommon at best in our waters, and, since it rarely comes inshore, it is a negligible hazard to California swimmers". It is now known that Great Whites will venture as far north as Nova Scotia (45°N).

Apart from the Great White, other sharks which have been known to make unprovoked attacks are the Mako, the Tiger, several of the Hammerheads and the Whalers of Australia. The Mako is one of the most active and strongest swimming of all sharks. A deep cobalt blue above and white below when viewed in its natural habitat, it is fine game fish and once it becomes hooked, it will leap repeatedly out of the water. The voluntary playful leaps it has been known to make 5m (15ft) into the air, could only be achieved by swimming at least 35km/h (22mph). The strongly swept back leading edges of the Mako's fins provide greater stream-lining to its body. It is said to reach 4m (13ft) long, although the maximum recorded length is 3.7m (12ft). The Atlantic Mako *Isurus oxyrinchus*, is also known as the Sharpnosed Mackerel Shark in the United States and South Africa, and as the Bonito on the west coast of the United States. Another of the species, *Isurus*

paucus, lives in the Indo-Pacific region and is known in Australia as the Blue Pointer.

Mako is a Maori name which once again, implies 'tooth'. In the north of New Zealand, the Maoris caught these sharks near the North Cape, working from canoes, and with fish as bait. When a shark came alongside the canoe, they would slip a noose over its head. If they had used hooks, they would have damaged the prized large central teeth, which were worn as ear ornaments. Of considerable value, it is reported that a pair of bullocks was the going exchange rate for a pair of shark's teeth in 1855! There are twelve to fourteen teeth on each side of the mouth in both the upper and lower jaw, which, unlike those of the Great White Shark, are smooth-edged.

Makos rarely move into water colder than 15°C (60°F). Their staple diet is mackerel and herring-like fish, and they have been seen chasing schools of these. Squid are probably another food item, while an almost intact 54kg (120lb) Swordfish (*Xiphias gladius*) was found in the stomach of a 330kg (730lb) Mako caught near Bimini.

Makos have a tendency to rush to the surface of the sea, in what appears to be an aggressive move to attack boats. Even though this can, and has, resulted in the smashing of a boat with the crew cast overboard, the sharks do not seem to attack man under these circumstances.

The Tiger Shark also known colloquially as the 'Tiger', is considered second only to the White Shark for ferocity. Its name arises not from its behaviour, but from the obviously striped juvenile stage, although the stripes almost disappear in the adult, leaving a uniform grey colour with faint stripey markings. Reaching an average length of 3.7-4.0m (12-13ft)—the record is 6.25m (20ft 10in)—the Tiger is one of the most numerous of the larger sharks, particularly in the tropical west Atlantic. It is a frequent visitor to the West Indies, although it is rarely seen near the surface of the water in the daytime. As darkness falls however, the plankton rises and small fish move up to feed, followed by larger fish and finally, at the end of the food chain, the Tiger Shark. Tiger Sharks move up the Atlantic coast of the United States, north of Florida, only during the summer and in the warmer Australian waters, they are responsible for many beach attacks.

The front and side teeth of a Tiger Shark are very large, and wickedly serrated on both edges, with an obvious notch on the outer edge. They are

capable of cutting through the shell of a sea turtle and an extracted tooth can effectively shave a man's fore-arm. Tiger Sharks are omnivorous and will eat anything they come across quite indiscriminately. Large conch shells, fishes, birds, crabs, including horseshoe crabs, squid, sting rays, sea lions, pieces of shark, as well as a leather wallet, a quantity of coiled copper wire, parts of dead dogs and sheep, tin cans, coal and sacks have all been found at various times in Tiger Shark stomachs. A complete 1.5m (5ft) long Hammerhead Shark was even found in one. It is well known that Tiger Sharks will bite chunks from other sharks, including their own species, which become emeshed in nets and they will also readily attack surface baits at night.

There are two famous accounts of Tiger Sharks eating man. One lived to tell the tale, the other was dead before the shark found part of his body. The first encounter took place in the Torres Strait between North Guinea and Australia where native pearl divers rarely miss seeing one shark a day and attacks are not uncommon. One diver survived the most incredible attack. He was first bitten on the head and then across the jaws and neck, at which stage, he somehow managed to squeeze the shark's eyes, until the fish released its grip and let go. The diver required almost 200 stitches to repair the two rows of teeth marks, and proof of the shark's identification came some weeks later, when inside an abscess which had developed on the man's neck, was the tooth of a Tiger Shark!

The other episode involving a Tiger Shark, sounds almost too far fetched to be part of a novel, let alone the true story it actually is. The year is 1935, the place Sydney, Australia. On 18th April, Albert Hobson, a fisherman, pulled in his line to discover he had caught two sharks—a 4.3m (14ft) Tiger which had almost eaten a smaller shark. Hobson managed, with assistance, to get the live Tiger ashore and to the Coogee Aquarium where for two days it lay almost motionless. Then it began to eat any food it was given until suddenly, four days later, it stopped eating and became seemingly lifeless again. On April 25th it suddenly swam in frantic circles, before regurgitating some of its stomach contents. Up to the surface floated the remains of a rat, a bird and, most macabre of all, a human arm with a rope around the wrist.

So began one of the strangest murder mysteries Australia, or indeed any country, has ever known. No other trace of human remains were found inside the shark and the top of the arm had in any event been cleanly cut with a knife, not rasped at by a shark's jaws. On it was a tattoo mark of two boxers. With painstaking care, fingerprints were

obtained from the shrivelled fingers by removing
the skin and these led police to the identification
of a missing person, who had indeed had a tattooed
left arm. He had last been seen some days before
18th April. Exactly what happened to him since,
was never established, however, for the rest of his
body was never found and police never gleaned
enough evidence to convict a man of his murder.
But for a greedy Tiger Shark, not even this much
would have come to light.

The Tiger Shark is a prolific breeder. Eighty two
foetuses were found inside a 4.8 m (14 ft 7 in) long
specimen, caught off Cuba, although thirty to
fifty young is a more usual number.

The sharks which have the most monster-like
appearance must surely be the Hammerheads. The
front of the head of these grotesque species is
flattened and enlarged on each side to form two
lobes. From above, these are shaped to look like a
T-bar and hence the name 'hammer' and 'bonnet'.
Hammerheads resemble a Carcharhinid shark with

a lobe on each side of its head. Both the eyes and
the nostrils are situated far apart, the eyes on the
outer edges of the lobes and the nostrils inside, but
well away from the midline. Several theories have
been put forward to explain these curious
extensions, although none have been proved con-
clusively. One suggests the head functions as a
hydroplane, thereby allowing the Hammerhead to
descend (or ascend) rapidly, but as Hammerheads
swim no faster than other sharks this is not borne
out in reality. A more recent, but unproven, theory
is that the widely spaced nostrils provide a
Hammerhead with a 'stereoscopic' sense of smell.

The Great Hammerhead (*Sphyrna mokarran*)
which has a world-wide distribution and usually
reaches 5 m (15 ft), is the largest of the species. Its
record length so far is 5.59 m (18 ft 4 in). The front
edge of the Great Hammerhead is almost a straight
line, while the Scalloped Hammerhead (*Sphyrna
lewini*), and Common Hammerhead (*Sphyrna
zygaena*) Sharks, both have a convex outline to

their heads, which is distinctly scalloped in the former. The smaller Bonnet or Shovel-nosed Hammerhead (*Sphyrna tiburo*), not surprisingly has a shovel-shaped head and between June and October, is the most abundant shark found off South Carolina. Young Hammerheads are born alive. Their hammer lobes are pliable at this stage, so that they are folded back as the sharks are born.

The largest species of Hammerheads, together with the Great White and Mako Sharks, are all given the highest rating in the US Navy 'Shark Danger' ratings. However, relatively few have attacked man. In 1805, parts of a man's body were found in one of three Hammerheads landed at Long Island, but there is no proof that the man was alive when he was eaten. A Hammerhead was known to kill a man in the Virgin Islands in 1963.

Large schools of Great Hammerheads migrate northwards up the Atlantic coast of North America in summer, but once the water falls below 19.5°C (67°F) they disappear. Their distri-

bution is quite widespread however, and in 1968, as RRS 'Discovery' was steaming at a speed of 10 knots into Dakar on the West African coast, members of the crew reported seeing about one Hammerhead per minute. They appear to feed over an extensive depth range, since pelagic and surface fish, as well as bottom living crabs have been found inside their stomachs. They are also cannabilistic, happy to eat their smaller relatives, particularly those unfortunates which have become caught in nets. One 4.3m (14ft) long Hammerhead was found to have almost finished eating six others. However the 'eat and be eaten' principle applies somewhat, for Hammerheads are frequently eaten themselves by other sharks after they have taken a baited line.

As in the Carcharhinid sharks, the third eyelid or nictitating membrane, is especially well developed in the Hammerheads. The value of this membrane is not at all clear however, more particularly as many sharks do not have one.

ABOVE Divers in the Red Sea escort a Hammerhead Shark (*Sphyrna zygaena*). This head-on view of the Hammerhead shows how its eyes are situated at the outer edge of each head lobe.

'Whaler' is the name used in Australia and New Zealand for several fierce sharks, which were renowned for attacking whale catches. The evidence now seems to point to the Tiger Shark and the Common or Black Whaler (*Carcharhinus macrurus*), which grows up to 4m (12ft) long, as being responsible for the majority of the shark attacks off the New South Wales coastline. The Whalers attack mainly in harbours and lagoons, while the Tigers menace the beaches.

Related to the Black Whaler are the White-tip Oceanic Shark (*Carcharhinus longimanus*) and the White-tip Reef Shark (*Carcharhinus platyrhynchus*). The oceanic species frequents warm open waters and seldom comes inshore, which has resulted in very little being known about its life and habits. It could be that it is an abundant shark, for several hundred were seen by the Woods Hole Oceanographic vessel 'Atlantis', 80 kilometres (50 miles) off the Massachusetts coast in June 1941. Growing to a record length of 3.5m (11ft 6in), they are reported to be languid swimmers. Yet they must be capable of a fair turn of speed, for five 6.5kg (15lb) tunas were found inside one specimen and tunas are renowned for their fast swimming ability. The White-tip Oceanic Shark, as its name implies, has white tips to its fins and its heterocercal tail, which has a distinctly large upper lobe. The accusations levelled at it, of being a man-eater, have little proof to substantiate them.

The White-tip Reef Sharks also have white-tipped fins and they have been observed to feed by making sudden rushes at their food, taking a bite and then moving away. When diving around Clipperton Island—an isolated shark-infested atoll 965 kilometres (600 miles) south west of Mexico—Dr. Limbaugh observed that these sharks were attracted by the green swimming fins of some divers, but not to brown or to black fins. Also present around Clipperton were large numbers of Galapagos Sharks (*Carcharhinus galapagensis*).

The Great Blue Shark or Bluedog, is one of the most beautiful of all the sharks. A black-indigo blue above and white beneath, it should not be confused with the Blue Sharks or Porbeagles (*Lamna* spp.). The Great Blue Shark is the most abundant large oceanic shark in the Atlantic, and it begins to move into shallow Californian waters when warm currents begin to flow into Monterey Bay. The record length for a Great Blue Shark is 3.8m (12ft 7in) and it is considered by sailors to be a man-eater. Game fishermen catch about 5000 of these sharks each year off Looe in Cornwall, where they are known simply as Blue Sharks. Examination of stomach contents of sharks caught in this fishery, show that they eat mostly small near-surface fish, such as herring and mackerel, as well as some squid and cuttlefish while occasional specimens have been found to have bottom living animals in their stomachs, including bivalve molluscs, worms and crabs. In addition the odd assortment of string, stones, polythene bags, paper, wood and aluminium foil revealed the usual indiscriminatory feeding nature of sharks. Two stomachs were even found to contain identifiable remains of dolphins, which may possibly give an indication of how individual sharks sometimes develop what appears to be an isolated taste for mammalian flesh. Pointing to stranger, or perhaps more exotic tastes still, in 1942, a trawler caught a 2m (6ft) Great Blue Shark, inside which was a bottle of old, but none the less apparently excellent, Madeira! Other records of flying fish and sea birds found among the stomach contents of specimens from warmer waters, would tend to indicate that Great Blue Sharks feed at the sea surface and indeed, they are often identified when basking at the surface, by their long pointed snouts and their long sickle-shaped pectoral fins.

Great Blue Sharks are viviparous, usually producing twenty-five to fifty or more young which are 38-46cm (15-18in) when they are born. The largest litters are generally produced by the females with the longest bodies.

In addition to these man-eating sharks already discussed, those found in Australian waters, with a similar reputation are the Sea or Bull Shark (*Carcharhinus leucas* (*C. gangeticus*)), the Grey Nurse Shark (*Odontaspis* (*Carcharias*) *arenarius*) and the Sand Shark (*Carcharias taurus*), which has been known to make unprovoked attacks in South African waters as well. More shark fatalities occur on the east side of Australia, in particular around Sydney, Newcastle, Townsville and the Torres Strait area, than anywhere else in the world. Shark attacks on man can occur at any time of the day, or night, but in Australia, the majority are documented as taking place between 3-6pm. Since shark nets were erected on the ocean beaches in the Sydney area in 1936, the only attacks in this area have been in unmeshed waters.

LEFT The term Whaler Shark is applied to several Australian *Carcharhinus* species. It was given to the sharks which attacked whale carcases being towed into Towfold Bay in the 1840's.

BELOW A White-Tip Shark (*Triaenodon obesus*) approaches menacingly close to a diver intent on filming it. There are, however, few authenticated attacks on man by this shark.

of Cancer; and from October to May, in a Southern Seasonal Zone, the same distance south of the Tropic of Capricorn.

The full impact of the potential danger of man-eating sharks was not appreciated until the early years of World War II, when many sailors and airmen survived being shot down or capsized, only to be attacked by sharks. It is known that less than half of the 450 men aboard a British warship torpedoed in the South Atlantic during World War II survived, but it is not known what percentage of the fatalities were torpedoed, drowned or attacked by sharks. When rescue ships arrived at the scene of another wartime disaster, many of the bodies found in their life-jackets were legless. As these kind of accounts became known, the morale of sailors and airmen working in known shark-infested areas understandably became very low, so to help boost morale, the US Naval Research Laboratory set to work to develop a shark repellent. They discovered that three substances—maleic acid, copper sulphate and decomposing

Lookout towers were also erected, for spotting sharks before they moved close inshore, and nothing empties the surfy waters of a Sydney beach quicker than a shark siren!

On a world scale, the shark attack belt is approximately 6500 kilometres (4000 miles) wide. The region between the Tropics of Cancer and Capricorn is potentially dangerous at all times of the year, although relatively few attacks take place near the equator. From April to November attacks may occur in a Northern Seasonal Zone 1930 kilometres (1200 miles) north of the Tropic

BELOW From the safety of a shark cage, divers watch a patrolling Great White Shark (*Carcharodon carcharias*). They have lured it closer with a bait, for study.

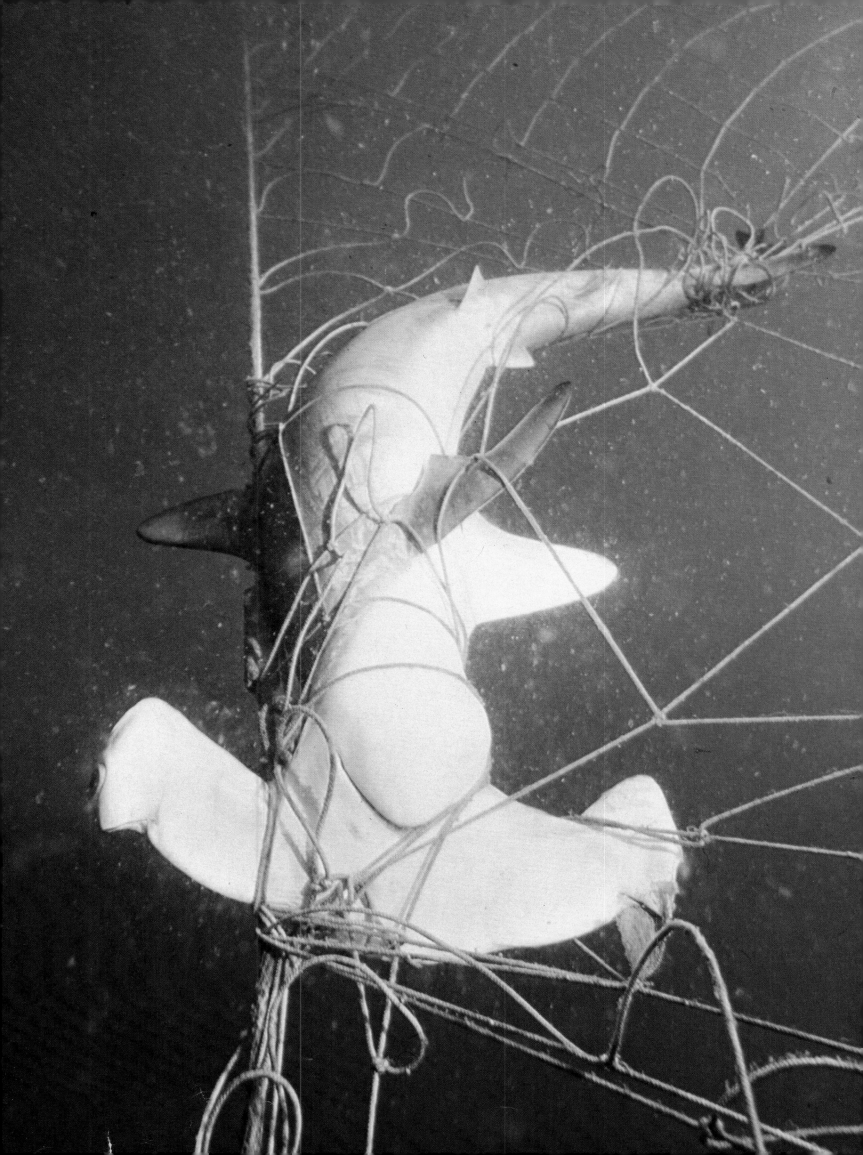

shark flesh (chiefly ammonium acetate)—showed positive repellent properties on captive sharks. From these experiments they developed tablets, known as "Shark Chasers", which contained twenty per cent copper acetate (the repellent component) and eighteen per cent purple nigrosine dye (the smoke screen similar to that produced by octopuses). Shark Chasers were issued to all personnel involved in operations on or above shark-infested waters, but the conflicting reports of their effectiveness as a deterrent will surely be no surprise to those of us now fully conversant with sharks' unpredictability. When they were tried out on packs of sharks attracted into waters discoloured with whale blood, some of the sharks were repelled, while others swam round in frenzied circles and ate the Chaser! Research along these lines continued, but so far seems only to have come up with the unsurprising result, that no shark repellent is infallible.

A curtain of air bubbles forming a 'bubble-barrier' has been considered as a possible shark deterrent in inshore waters, although the fact that some sharks pass straight through it must make its effectiveness debatable! In experiments conducted at Bimini, only one Tiger Shark out of twelve was turned back by a bubble curtain. Other methods of protection against dangerous sharks are physical barriers which prevent contact with man. Shark cages, such as those used by Cousteau and others like him, are 'human zoos', which enable biologists and photographers to observe and photograph sharks in comparative safety while remaining at close quarters.

The three main countries to have their shores washed by shark-infested water—the United States of America, Australia and South Africa—are now involved in research into man-eaters. Fishermen and divers, as well as doctors and biologists, are pooling all their information about the habits and behaviour of man-eating sharks. In 1958 a Shark Research Panel was founded in the United States, and it has built up a world-wide Shark Attack File (SAF) in which each recorded attack was given a specific number. Shark Panels have also been formed in Australia and South Africa.

Data from 1952 attacks in the SAF have been subjected to computer analysis, in an attempt to determine the existence, or absence, of common factors associated with shark attacks on man. Amongst the conclusions scientist, David Baldridge, drew from this research programme, was the reiteration that the odds of being attacked by a shark, in sea water with a temperature below 20-21°C (68-70°F), were very slight. However, in warmer waters, the odds of being attacked in shallow water were high, since sixty two per cent of the 470 cases where the depth was recorded

in the File, were attacked in water less than 1.5 m (5 ft) deep. There also seems to be a distinct sex discrimination. A very high proportion (just over ninety three per cent) of attacks were made on males. It could be argued that more men than women, by nature of such occupations as seamen, and fishermen, are susceptible to attack, but even when the attacks on swimmers only at, or near beaches, were analyzed, the percentage was still high showing a ratio of over nine males to one female. In general male swimmers are naturally more active than women in the water and it is thought that they may also give off a more attractive body odour than females—to sharks, at least! It should be pointed out this fact is far from proven!

One fifth of the records in the SAF are of attacks on divers, who tend to believe that totally submerged people are less likely to be attacked by a shark than a swimmer at the surface. Diving however, is a relatively recent sport and over seventy-five per cent of all the attacks on divers in the SAF took place after 1950. During the period 1950-9, twenty-five per cent of all attacks recorded in the File were made on divers. This was a much higher percentage than would be reasonable to expect from the ratio of divers to bathers. As the percentage of attacks on divers continues to increase, it appears that, contrary to popular belief, divers are more—and not less—likely to be attacked by sharks than swimmers.

There are numbers of carnivorous sharks, which are not renowned man-eaters, but will nevertheless attack if they are provoked. Amongst these are the Nurse and Carpet Sharks, which belong to the same family as the Wobbegongs of Australia. The Nurse Shark (*Ginglymostoma cirratum*)—not to be confused with the Australian Grey Nurse Shark (*Carcharias arenarius*)—has a reputation for being 'harmless', even though it has been known to attack swimmers. It has a short snout with an almost terminal mouth and a barbel or feeler emanates from the front margin of each nostril. Nurse Sharks grow to a length of about 4.3 m (14 ft) and the large, closely packed scale teeth on their outer skin, make an effective barrier against harpoon guns. They live in tropical inshore waters and divers frequently encounter them off

BELOW The Tawny Shark (*Ginglymostoma ferrugineum*) is a nocturnal bottom feeding shark. It has small eyes. Just in front of its mouth, sensory barbels arise close to the openings of its nostrils.

BELOW Seen from beneath, this Sand Shark (*Ginglymostoma brevicaudatum*) clearly shows the two barbels just in front of its mouth, and its broad pectoral fins, which act like aquaplanes.

BOTTOM A Nurse or Sleeper Shark (*Ginglymostoma cirratum*) rests on the sea-bed. The small eye and sensory barbels near the mouth are typical features of bottom-feeding nocturnal species.

RIGHT The colouration of this Carpet Shark or Wobbegong (*Orectolobus ogilbyi*), coupled with its fringed head outline, helps it to blend in with pale sandy bottoms of its natural environment.

Florida and the West Indies. It is provocation by divers, such as tail-grabbing, which has induced several of the known attacks by Nurse Sharks of all sizes from 45 cm-2.7 m (18 in-9 ft). Observation accounts of Nurse Sharks mating are not uncommon. The male apparently grasps the hind edge of one of the female's pectoral fins, turns her on to her back and inserts his claspers. Nurse Sharks are ovoviviparous.

The beautiful mottled colouring of the Wobbegongs, a name coined from the aborigines, disrupts the body outline and thereby camouflages these sharks so they can blend in with the weeds and rocks on the ocean bottom. Further camouflage is afforded by the fringe of fleshy barbels around the mouth. The largest of the three species of Wobbegongs is *Orectolobus maculatus*, which grows to 3.2 m (10 ft 6 in) long. These sharks were another of the species reputed to be harmless, until that is, one bit the foot of a fisherman who stepped on it!

ABOVE A Carpet Shark or Wobbegong (*Orectolobus maculatus*) resting 5m (16ft) down on an Australian shore.

ABOVE RIGHT The Greenland or Sleeper Shark (*Somniosus microcephalus*) is the only shark known to inhabit polar seas throughout the year.

RIGHT Wobbegong sharks are peaceable bottom-livers. However there are several records of attacks on bathers or divers who have inadvertently stepped on one.

As mentioned at the beginning of this chapter, not all sharks live in tropical or temperate waters. The Greenland or Sleeper Shark (*Somniosus microcephalus*), for example, ranges both sides of the Atlantic, and is the only shark which lives in polar waters throughout the year. In the winter it comes right up to the Arctic ice, but it can also survive in water temperatures as warm as 11°C (53°F). The average length of the Greenland Shark is 2.4-4.3m (8-14ft) and the record length is 6.4m (21ft). Even the large sized specimens are comparatively easily caught, as demonstrated by the Eskimos, who catch them on a hand line from a kayak. The Eskimos also lure the sharks up to the surface in order to harpoon them, by dripping blood into the water through a hole in the ice.

The Greenland Shark is caught primarily for its liver oil. Its skin is tough, like all sharkskin or shagreen, but it is treated in Denmark to remove the tips of the outer placoid scales. It can then be used to make various forms of clothing.

The name Sleeper Sharks arose from their reputation for living a lethargic life on the bottom of the ocean, but the evidence provided by their stomach contents, seems to suggest that they must be quite active predators. They are also known as

the Gurry Shark, from the nautical version of garbage, because of their habit of eating the refuse from fishing, whaling and sealing stations. Other food consists of a variety of fishes, crabs, seals, porpoises and sea birds.

The Thresher Shark (*Alopias vulpinus*), also known as the Fox Shark, Sea Fox, Swingletail, Thrasher and Whip-Tailed Shark, has a huge scythe-like tail which can be as long as the rest of its body. The record length for this species of Thresher Shark is 5.9m (18ft), and it is found in both temperate and tropical waters of all oceans. Compared with other sharks, both the jaws and the teeth of the Thresher Shark are relatively weak, but this is more than compensated by its oversized tail. This it uses to thresh the water and herd herring or mackerel and sometimes several Threshers will work together to herd the fish into a tight mass. Then the sharks make for the centre of the mass with wide open jaws, and gorge themselves on all this concentrated food. Threshers can also use their tail to stun sea birds on the surface of the sea.

The blunt-headed Port Jackson Shark (*Heterodontus portjacksoni*) of Australian waters, has changed little in appearance from its ancestors that lived in the Triassic era. It has a spine in front of

each of its two dorsal fins. The alternative name of Oyster Crusher, is derived from its habit of eating molluscs and sea urchins, which it grasps by the small cone-like incisors in the front of the mouth and crushes with plate-like molars at the back. There are several species of *Heterodontus* which are collectively known as Horn or Bullhead Sharks.

Amongst some of the more primitive sharks, are species with more than the usual five gill slits. The largest and most abundant of these is the six-gilled Cow Shark (*Hexanchus griseus*), which tends to occur in deep cool water, where it feeds at the bottom on fish, crustaceans, and any dead animals, including dead whales. There is a record of one Cow Shark having a complete torpedo in its stomach. Bathers at Nice might well be alarmed if they knew they were sharing the idyllic bay with sharks that can reach a size of 8 m (26 ft 5 in)! Even the 5 m (15 ft) specimens weigh nearly 600 kg (1320 lbs). The characteristic comb-shape teeth of Cow Sharks, have been found in Middle Jurassic deposits of 150 million years ago.

The seven-gilled sharks are much rarer and usually frequent deeper water. However, the Narrow-headed Seven-gilled Shark (*Heptranchias perlo*) has been found in deep water off Cuba as well as the shallow roadsteads along tropical West Africa. It is also found off Australia and in the Mediterranean. Its maximum size is 2.14 m (7 ft), whereas the Broad-headed Seven-gilled Shark (*Notorhynchus maculatus*), found in the Indo-Pacific, is bigger and grows over 3 m (10 ft) long. Both species are fish eaters.

I have left describing the two largest sharks to the end of the chapter, as they are both plankton feeders. Beached carcasses of the Basking Shark, however, have led to more than one story of 'a Monster of the Deep'. After death, the lower jaw and body cavity rot away leaving behind a tiny brain case, a long backbone and the remains of the fins, which collectively resemble a sea serpent. In 1970, local police in Massachusetts reported a sea serpent which looked like 'a giant camel without legs'. It turned out to be a Basking Shark.

Basking sharks have tiny teeth, but huge gill slits which almost meet above and below the throat. Inside the gill arches, are the stiff bristle-like gill rakers. These Sharks feed—often near the surface—by gathering plankton into their huge mouths and filtering it on these gill rakers. A 7 m (23 ft) long Basking Shark, cruising at a speed of 2 knots, strains about 1,800,000 kg (4,000,000 lb) of seawater in an hour and inside the stomach of one Basking Shark, 136 kg (300 lb) of plankton was found. At the onset of winter, when the plankton level drops, the shark sheds its gill rakers and moves down into deeper water, until the plankton levels increase in the following spring. At this time, it regrows its gill rakers.

The record size for a Basking Shark is 13.7 m (45 ft) and the estimated weight of this one was 14,500 kg (32,000 lb). Large specimens have been seen to leap right out of the sea, possibly in an attempt to get rid of parasites on their bodies. Basking Sharks are fished for their liver oil off

Ireland, where they are known as *muldoans*; in the Orkneys they are known as Hoe-mother or Homer, meaning the mother of the dogfish.

Both the Basking Shark and the Whale Shark, have large livers which acts as a buoyancy organ and thereby allows them to linger at the surface. An average sized Whale Shark is 10.7 m (35 ft) long and weighs 10 tonnes, while the record size is a staggering 18 m (59 ft). Thus the Whale Shark is *the* monster of all sharks known to be alive today. The upper surface of its grey or brownish body is dotted with white or yellow spots, while the underside is white or yellow. Its mouth is situated at the front of its head and it has conspicuous ridges running along each side of the body. It also has the distinction of possessing the thickest skin of any living animal; a 9.1 m (30 ft) long whale was found to have skin 10 cm (2.5 in) thick.

Because of their vast size, Whale Sharks are difficult to weigh accurately, but the estimated weight of the record specimen is 41,000 kg (90,000 lb). These sharks, which frequent the warmer parts of the Atlantic, Pacific and Indian Oceans, are comparatively rare and only about ninety have been recorded by marine biologists. One 9.8 m (32 ft) long Whale Shark was finally beached at Mangalore in India in 1959, after it had been hooked through its dorsal fin and had towed two steel boats of 9.7 m and 8.2 m (32 and 27 ft) long—plus their occupants—at a speed of 5 knots for 20 minutes.

By the nature of their feeding habits, Basking and Whale Sharks are both considered to be 'inoffensive'. However, there are several reports of ships colliding with Whale Sharks basking at the surface, such as a famous one in 1934, when a Whale Shark collided so violently with the liner 'Mauragnui' in the South Pacific, that it was impaled on the bow.

Rays and Giant Fishes

Rays belong to the same family as sharks, but they in no way evoke the same fear and respect in man. In many ways this is a misconception, for several species of rays are extremely dangerous—the pernicious sting of the sting rays has been known to kill a man, and the electric or torpedo rays are capable of delivering severe electric shocks. The colloquial names bestowed on rays in various parts of the world—Devil fish, Eagle Ray, Shark Ray and Sawfish—do indicate that some people at least, have long been aware of the potential menace and danger of these fish.

The vast majority of the 350 species of ray spend most of their time on the seabed, where they scavenge and feed on worms and molluscs from the sand and mud. Like their shark relatives, they have a cartilaginous skeleton and their characteristic flattened shape is an adaption to life on the bottom. Their enlarged triangular pectoral fins are developed rather like wings and the rays swim by undulations passing down them. Their long, whip like tail is of little use for swimming, and instead, is modified into a defensive organ. In the stingrays and some eagle rays, it carries a large, evil, saw-edged spine near its base. Ray's gill slits are on the underside of their body, and on the top of the head, just behind the eyes, are a pair of openings called spiracles. Water is drawn through the spiracles, passed over the gills and out of the gill slits beneath the body, so that a ray resting on the muddy ocean bottom can get a supply of clean water to its gills, while barely disturbing the surrounding area. Like many fish, rays are masters of camouflage and the mottled coloration on the backs of several species, enables them to merge in with the sea-bed. They complete their disguise still further, by flipping a little sand and mud up over the edge of their bodies as they come to rest.

The mouth of most rays is situated on the underside of the body and the type of teeth they possess provides a clue to their normal diet. Rays that feed on molluscs, for example, usually have pavement teeth, which they use to grind and crush the shells.

As with sharks, there are few hard and fast features common to all species of ray. The largest of them all, the Giant Devil or Manta (*Manta birostris*), is the first to break the generalization of the ray's mouth being situated on the underside of its body. Instead, this ray has its mouth on the front of its head, and the two horn-like projections which flank it, can be turned over the front. It is thought the Manta uses them to herd and funnel food into its mouth.

The Manta Ray is a giant indeed and the largest specimen of this tropical species so far recorded, was caught in the Bahamas. It was 6.7 m (22 ft) across its pectoral fins and 5.2 m (17 ft) long, but as part of its tail was missing, even this is not its true length. It weighed a staggering 1360 kg (nearly 3000 lb).

Like so many giants of the sea—the Blue Whale, the Whale Shark and the Basking Shark—these rays are plankton feeders. Normally they are placid, if somewhat curious, beasts, but when harpooned, their immense strength is unleashed and they are quite capable of capsizing boats. Their strength is also shown when they leap clear of the water. The reason for this leaping behaviour is not known, but it is thought it may be associated with mating. The tremendous booming crash as they belly-flop back into the water, can be heard like a clap of thunder from a great distance away and it might be a "come and get it" signal to a prospective mate. The sight of one of these giants leaping from the ocean is awesome indeed, and it is no wonder that superstitious natives attributed all manner of evil to these rays. Pearl divers believed that Mantas were capable of folding their great wings around a man, to hold him as they devoured him—a belief which is happily disproved by an examination of a Manta's teeth. The upper jaw is toothless; the lower one carries numerous tiny flattened teeth. After all what more do you need if you live on a diet of plankton soup?

Mantas are usually seen at the surface of the sea, swimming along with their wing-tips just breaking the water. Below water, they are a most graceful sight; but they can be a danger to divers, who could easily be bowled over by their very strong backwash. Mantas are fertilized internally. The anal fins of the males are modified into claspers which they use to fertilize the females.

More dangerous than the Mantas are the torpedo or electric rays' which produce the most powerful shocks amongst the electric marine fishes. As sea water is a better conductor of electricity than freshwater, it is not necessary for marine electric fishes to generate such high voltages to stun their prey. Electric rays have small eyes and small mouths, and are found in both tropical and temperate seas. Most live on the bottom in shallow water close inshore. They are ovoviviparous; the eggs hatch inside the mother who gives birth to live young.

BELOW LEFT A silhouetted Eagle Ray (*Aetobatus narinari*) glides through the water. The spine of this sting ray is situated at the point where the whip tail arises from the base of the body.

BELOW The Manta Ray (*Manta birostris*) feeds on plankton, and the huge mouth lobes are used to funnel plankton towards the large mouth slit. Notice the eye at the base of the right mouth lobe.

One of the largest is *the* Electric Ray (*Torpedo nobiliana*), which grows to approximately 2m (6ft) long and has an almost circular, or disc-shaped, body. The shock it produces can certainly unbalance a man, and a discharge of 220 volts has been measured from one specimen. Known to feed on several different kinds of fish, it leaps onto its prey, and wraps its pectoral fins around it, while discharging an immobilizing current from its electric organs. These consist of specialized muscles contained in two large and two small organs on each side of its head and the current passes from the upper (positive) side of the fish to the lower (negative) side.

Another species of electric ray, *Torpedo torpedo*, lives in the east part of the Atlantic and also in the Mediterranean. On the top side of its body are five conspicuous blue spots encircled with black and then white. In contrast to the mottled camouflage colour of most other rays, these conspicuous blue circles actually advertize the ray's presence,

warning would-be attackers of the potential dangers in provoking it. In this way, the ray is left undisturbed, while its enemies look elsewhere for food.

The largest of all the marine sting rays belong to the family Dasyatidae. The bodies of these long fish are angular, as opposed to the rounded shape of the electric rays, and they possess no dorsal or tail fins. They are armed with a deadly weapon however—a serrated spine with venom filled grooves running along its base, and this is situated on top and towards the front of their long whip-like tails. If a diver inadvertently treads on a sting ray, the fish instantly flexes its tail upwards, stabbing its spine into the offending foot or leg. The wound thus produced is always painful and can be sufficient to kill a man. Indo-Pacific natives are known to use the spines from sting rays in making their daggers and spear tips.

Most sting rays live in warm tropical waters, but some will move up in to temperate waters

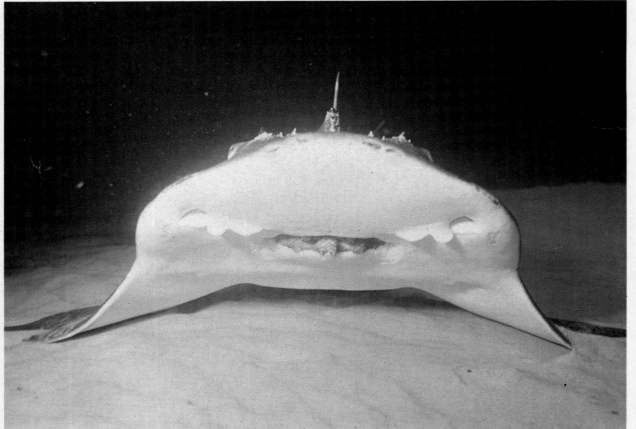

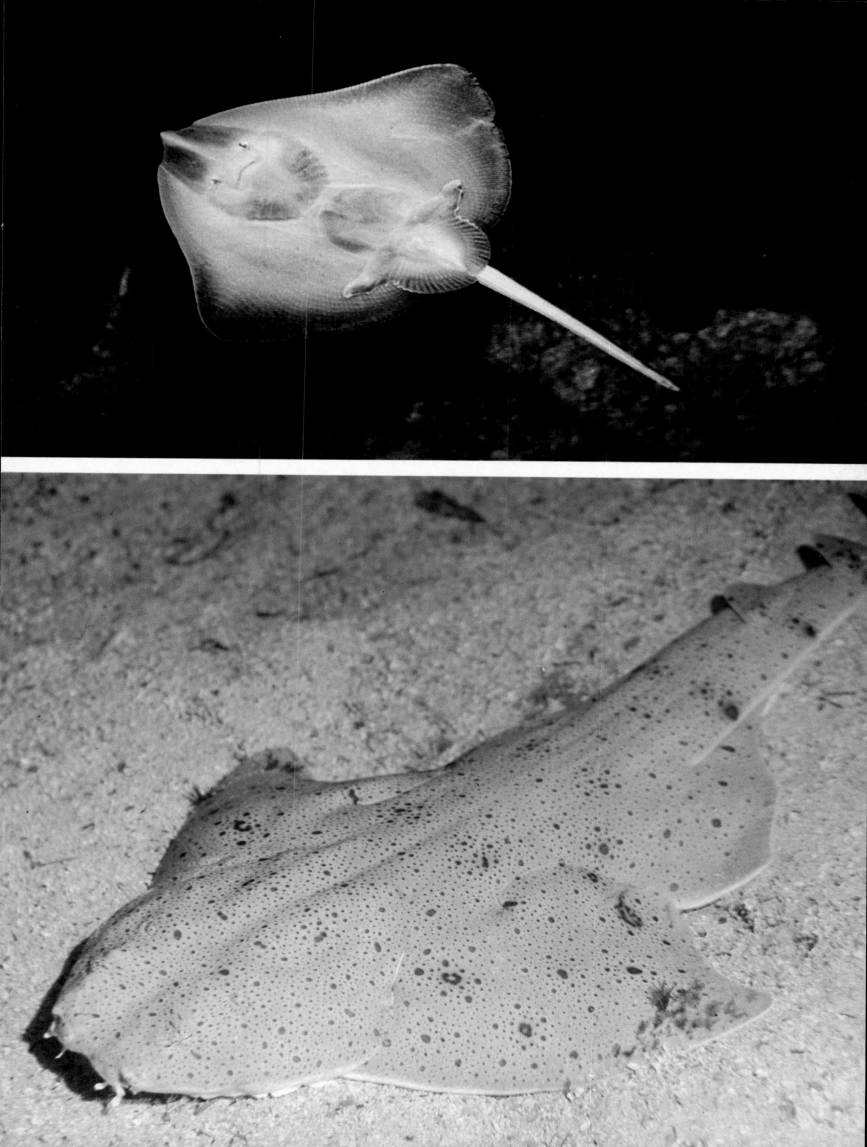

BELOW A Manta Ray (*Manta birostris*) swims over a coral reef. Travelling with it are ten or more Remoras or shark suckers. These suckers hitch a ride over long distances.

RIGHT A skin diver swims down to a Manta Ray which is swimming head-on towards the camera. From each corner of the mouth, a curved horn projects downwards.

BELOW CENTRE Groupers (*Epinephelus spp.*) are large bony fish which live amongst rocks and crevices on rocky bottoms. This one shows the typical huge wide lipped mouth.

BOTTOM RIGHT The Manta or Giant Devil Ray (*Manta birostris*) is the largest of all rays. Like the Eagle Ray, it has a dark upper surface and a white belly.

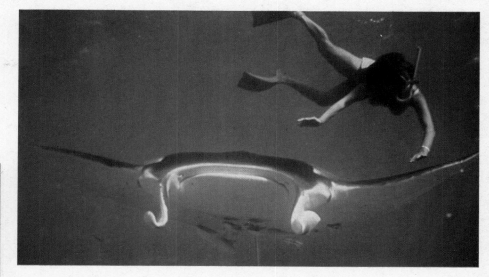

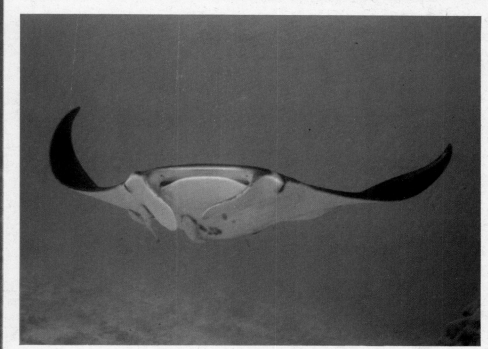

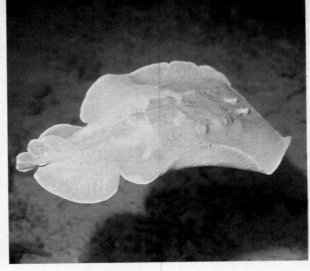

during the summer months. They live on the bottom, feeding on shellfish, which they crush with their flattened teeth, and they can cause havoc amongst commercial shellfish beds.

The largest known sting ray is *Dasyatis brevicaudata*, which can be up to 4.3m (14ft) long and between 1.8 and 2.1m (6-7ft) wide. It lives in the Indo-Pacific region, where it frequents shallow waters around reefs and penetrates up estuaries. It shares this habitat with a spectacular sting ray—the Blue-Spotted Sting Ray or Ribbontail Ray (*Taeniura lymma*). The flat ribbon-like tail of this ray is longer than the rest of its creamy coloured body, which is covered in an array of blue spots (see overleaf).

Some of the eagle rays also have a poisonous tail spine. These rays are active mid-water swimmers and use their long pointed pectoral fins to move elegantly through tropical and warm temperate waters. They have a more obvious head region than other sting rays, as their pectoral fins stop short, level with the eyes. One of the best known species, the Spotted Eagle Ray (*Aetobatus narinari*), reaches a length of 2.36m (7ft 9in) and a width of more than 2m (6ft). Its serrated spine is situated at the base of its whip-like tail. The Spotted Eagle

Ray also feeds on commercially important shell-fish, including clams and oysters, which it crushes with its flat pavement-like teeth.

The elongate sawfishes are related to the rays and their gill slits are similarly situated on the underside of their head. Their somewhat shark-shaped bodies have a blade-like snout, or 'saw', which has strong teeth on either side, gradually diminishing in size as they near the head. The fish appears to use its saw to stir up the ocean bed in order to find the invertebrates on which it feeds. It may also use it to procure a meal, by lashing into passing shoals of fish, and saw teeth have even been found embedded in the insulation of sub-marine cables. As with the spines of the sting ray, native islanders use the saw from sawfish as a highly efficient weapon. The Greater Sawfish (*Pristis pectinata*) reaches a length of 7.7m (25ft) and has twenty four to thirty two pairs of teeth along its saw.

Close relatives of the sawfish, the saw sharks, also have an elongated snout, but alternately small and large teeth grow along it. When the young are born, their teeth are folded within the skin, but they begin to emerge soon after birth. In addition, saw sharks have long barbels projecting from

ABOVE LEFT The elongated whip-like tail, typical of most stingrays, is clearly seen in this Atlantic Sting Ray (*Dasyatis sabina*).

ABOVE The short stubby tail projects only a short distance beyond the body of this Electric Ray.

RIGHT These embryonic Electric Rays (*Torpedo marmorata*) are miniatures of their parent, although at this stage, their eyes are much more conspicuous against their pale, unpigmented body.

BELOW A Southern Sting Ray (*Dasayatis americana*) is widespread in the Caribbean. Along its back is a row of bony tubercles.

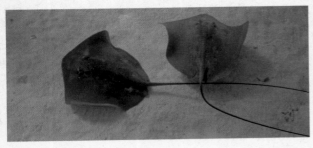

LEFT A pair of Black Sting Rays entwine their tails as they court over the bottom at Saumarez Reef. Notice the way the edges of the pectoral lobes undulate up and down.

RIGHT The Blue Spotted Sting Ray (*Taeniura lymma*) is one of the more exotic patterned sting rays to inhabit the Indo-Pacific. It is also known as the Ribbontail Ray.

LEFT Eagle Rays are widely distributed in the tropical seas where they can sometimes be seen splashing in the shallows of sandy bays as they are mating.

beneath each side of the snout, which they use to detect their bottom-living food. The Common Saw Shark (*Pristiophorus cirratus*), frequents the Indo-Pacific region and grows to a length of 1.2 m (4 ft).

The guitarfishes exhibit both shark and ray features. The stout tail is not clearly separated from the body, which is often elongated, but, like rays, it is flattened for adaptation to life on the bottom. The gill slits are also on the underside of its body. Commonly used names for these fish are Fiddle Sharks and Shovel-nose Sharks.

All the fishes so far described in this book have a cartilaginous skeleton, but in fact the majority of fish, found both in the sea and freshwater, are bony fishes or teleosts. Some of these are important commercial fish (Cod and Herring); some are well known to fly fishermen and anglers (Trout and Salmon; Pike, Perch, Carp and Roach); while others are popular with aquarists (Cichlids, Tetras, Gouramis etc.). Teleosts have an internal bony skeleton and the skin is covered with rounded scales instead of the sharp placoid (or tooth-like) denticles of sharks. The five gill slits are hidden below a gill cover known as the operculum, which is used by the fish, not only to protect the delicate gills, but also to help with the pumping of water across them.

None of these fish can really be described as monsters, for what is thought to be the largest teleost amongst both marine and freshwater habitats, reaches a mere 4 m (13 ft) in length! This is the Blue-fin Tuna or Tunny (*Thunnus thynnus*) which lives in tropical and warm temperate waters of the Atlantic Ocean. Tagged Blue-fins have been known to cross from the American coast to European waters, and they are often seen breaking the surface as they feed on shoaling fish, which attempt to escape by leaping out of the water.

The Blue-fin Tuna is one of the fastest fish in the sea, and can reach a speed of 69 km/h (43.4 mph). The ability of tunnies to swim so fast is the product of several physiological adaptations. The body is highly stream-lined and rather rigid, and maybe stream-lined still further by withdrawing the dorsal, pectoral and pelvic fins into grooves. The vigorous tail beats, and flexing of the body generates and stores elastic energy, which is released as the tail straightens. This drives the fish through the water as well as re-inforcing the power of its muscles, which, in any event, contract at an increased rate, as the tunny is partly warm blooded. Red muscles, rich in the respiratory pigment, myoglobin, run down the length of the fish's body and they store oxygen needed when the tunny is swimming flat out. These muscles are often 10°C (18°F) warmer than the surrounding sea water, and the blood supply has a counterflow system so that the heat generated by the muscles' activity is conserved.

The heaviest bony fish in the world is the Ocean Sunfish (*Mola mola*). This bizarre fish has an almost circular body with no tail, and its elongated dorsal and anal fins are positioned towards the rear of its body. On average, an adult Ocean Sunfish measures 2 m (6 ft) from its snout to the edge of its tail fin and 2.6 m (8 ft) between the tips of its dorsal and anal fins and it can weigh up to 1 tonne. There are reports of larger specimens, but few have been authenticated with accurate measurements. So far the largest Sunfish known was one caught up in a ship's propeller off Sydney, Australia. It was taken ashore where it was measured at 3 m (10 ft) long, 4.3 m (14 ft) wide and weighed at 2.23 tonnes. The Ocean Sunfish is also the most prolific egg-producer; the ovaries inside one female were estimated as containing 300 million 1.2 mm (0.05 in) diameter eggs.

Other examples of impressive bony fish are the marlins, sailfish and the Swordfish (*Xiphias gladius*), all of which have a long pointed upper jaw or bill. This is flattened in the Swordfish and rounded in the marlin and sailfish, also known as billfish, and is thought to be used to stun smaller fish before they are eaten. Swordfish and billfish are often caught by harpooning, and as they are drawn aboard, they are liable to stab their bill into the hull of the boat. Such attacks are clearly provoked, but an attack made by a Swordfish at 600m (1968 ft) down on the American submersible 'Alvin', is inexplicable. In this instance the Swordfish had wedged its bill so tightly into the side of the craft, it was unable to withdraw it. Going back for more than a century, there is another amazing account of a Swordfish attack on a vessel. The stump of a bill was found projecting from the hull of the American whaling ship 'Fortune' when she returned to Massachusetts in 1826. The bill had pierced the outer copper sheathing and entered 2.5cm (1in) thick board sheathing, a 7.5cm (3in) wooden plank, a 30cm (12in) thick oak timber and a 6cm (2.5in) thick oak plank before penetrating an oak cask. In another more recent account, three dead Swordfish were washed ashore on the South African coast in May 1947—minus their swords. The mystery of the missing swords was soon solved however, when they were found buried in a rubber bale. They had penetrated so far into the side, that the fish were unable to withdraw them and so had eventually died. All this time, their bills would have snapped away from the fishes bodies.

Swordfish are active swimmers, able to reach speeds of 56-64km/h (35-40mph) in the warm temperate waters they frequent. They have no pelvic fins and no teeth, although they feed off a variety of fish and squid. The only natural predators Swordfish encounter are a few species of shark, but until recently at least, man has hunted large numbers, landing some 20,000 each year off the North American Atlantic coast. Recent reports of Swordfish containing high levels of mercury, has led to the virtual collapse of the fishery, because of consumer resistance.

The largest of the marlins is the Blue Marlin (*Makaira nigricans*), which reaches 4.6m (15ft) long. Found in tropical and warm temperate waters the world over, it is the most heavily exploited species and large numbers are caught each year in the Pacific, especially off Hawaii. The Black or White Marlin (*Makaira indica*) which grows to a length of 3.7m (12ft) is one of the fastest swimmers of all marine fishes.

The 3.6m (12ft) long Sailfish (*Istiophorus platypterus*), is related to the marlins, and in addition to the long bill, it has a high dorsal fin— the sail. This fin is bright blue, while the upper part of the fish's body is dark blue and the sides and belly, a whitish colour. Like other billfish, it is a favourite quarry amongst game fishermen, and when caught, its spectacular leaps out of the water make for a good fight.

Although not amongst the largest of marine fish, the barracuda's evil reputation earn it a place amongst the 'monsters of the deep'. Barracuda frequent shallow waters in tropical and warm temperate seas and their large jaws and sharp teeth indicate their notorious predatory habits. The Great Barracuda (*Sphyraena barracuda*), which reaches 1.8m (6ft) long, is more feared than sharks off the West Indies, and not surprisingly, for it has been known to make several attacks on swimmers, particularly in murky waters. Any disturbance in the water—even gentle splashing— may provoke an attack. In the West Indies barracuda flesh from some islands causes a poisoning called ciguatera, if it is eaten. This is identical to that caused by eating puffer, box and file fish and it is thought that barracuda eat these fish, and then accumulate the poisons in their own flesh.

The snake-like bodies and ever-gaping sharply toothed jaws of the moray eels, have combined to give them a similar evil reputation. It is perhaps less warranted than the barracuda's however, for these eels rarely make unprovoked attacks. When disturbed from their hide-outs amongst tropical reefs of temperate rocky faces, they nevertheless

ABOVE As an Eagle Ray (*Aetobatus narinari*) swims past, with an upward sweep of its pectoral fins, its five gill slits can be seen on the underside near its head end.

ABOVE CENTRE A pair of Small Toothed or Greater Sawfish (*Pristis pectinata*) rest on the ocean bottom. The regular pairs of teeth along the snout or 'saw' can be seen in the bottom shadow.

ABOVE FAR RIGHT A diver is surrounded by a shoal of "Jacks"—the colloquial name given to a family of fast-swimming predatory fish, well-known as hard-fighting sporting fishes.

RIGHT Spotted Eagle Rays (*Aetobatus narinari*) with three Remora suckers in the Red Sea. The marked variation in colouration of the upper and lower surfaces is seen here.

BELOW A Moray Eel (*Muraena* sp.) emerges from a coral reef hideout it shares with long-spined sea urchins. The black and white spotted pattern is a warning colouration.

BOTTOM A large school of barracuda (*Sphyraena* sp.) at Cape San Lucas. The vertical bands on the upper parts of the body help to break up the outline of these fish.

BELOW CENTRE This line up of five barracuda (*Sphyraena sp.*) hunting like a wolf pack, resemble an aeronautic formation. Barracudas are much-prized sporting fish.

RIGHT When an Ocean Sunfish (*Mola mola*) swims at the surface, its dorsal fin moves through the water with a slow sideways motion. Its body is almost circular.

FAR RIGHT A Moray Eel (*Muraena melanotis*) emerges from its hideout. The sharp pointed teeth of the upper jaw can be seen inside its ever-gaping mouth.

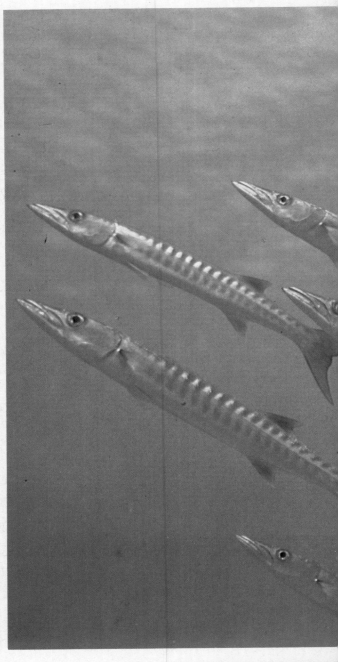

can be dangerously aggressive, and if they are cornered, they will inflict savage bites on their attacker. Anyone who ventures out on the reefs during low tide at night may also find themselves hunted by morays and the crew of the 'Kon Tiki' raft were chased from a lagoon by moray eels when their raft became wrecked on a Pacific atoll.

Moray eels breathe by continuously drawing in fresh supplies of sea water, which they pump over the gills, so they appear to be continually panting. For this reason, they have to swallow their food rapidly. The bold patterned bodies of several species of morays have given rise to the nickname 'painted eels'—a title certainly earned by species, *Lycodontis tesselata*, which is found in Indo-Pacific waters and has a striking body pattern. It grows to a length of 1.5m (5ft) and emerges at night from its hide-out to hunt over the reefs for fish and crabs. Like the moray eel, *Muraena helena*, found in the Mediterranean and eastern Atlantic, *Lycodontis tesselata*, and other tropical morays have an elongated body with no pelvic or pectoral fins. The Romans considered moray eels a delicacy, and served them as a special banquet dish. We are told 6000 morays were eaten at one banquet given by Caesar. The eels were kept in special fish reservoirs, called piscinas, close to the sea, and were apparently fed on the bodies of dead slaves.

Baleen or Whalebone Whales

The ocean's biggest inhabitants are the whalebone whales and the biggest of them all is the Blue Whale (*Balaenoptera musculus*). Growing to a length of 33 m (100 ft)—the actual record so far is 33.58 m (110 ft 2½ in)—it is the largest living animal and quite probably the largest animal that has ever lived. When a female of a mere 27.3 m long was weighed, she scaled 135 tonnes. The enormity of the Blue Whale perhaps becomes most apparent when it is seen in the context of a 20 m (63 ft) *Brontosaurus* which probably weighed about 30 tonnes and *Branchiosaurus*, the largest of the dinosaurs, which probably tipped the scales at around 50 tonnes. Even the tongue of the Blue Whale weighs 4 tonnes, which is the approximate weight of the largest terrestrial animal living today—the elephant. Animals of the size of the whalebone whales could only exist in an aquatic environment where the great body mass is supported by the surrounding water.

Like the elephant, whales are warm blooded mammals, giving birth to live young which are suckled on milk by the mother. Their fish-like shape led early naturalists to class them with fish, even though they cannot breathe underwater. Instead must surface to breathe air, and as they surface, they exhale through the blow-hole on the top of their head. The blow may be a single or a double one and, together with its angle, can be used by experts to identify certain species of whales when spotted at sea.

Apart from the hairs or vibrissae on their snout, whales have done away with the typically hairy mammalian coat to make way for a more streamlined body. They have no neck region, instead the outline of the head runs on as a continuous line with the body. The paddle-like fore arms are not separated into digits and whales also have no apparent hind limbs, although vestiges remain internally as rudimentary pelvic bones. The two horizontal lobes or flukes at the end of the whale's tail are used to propel the mammal through the

water. Beneath the skin, the blubber—a thick layer of fatty tissue containing cells filled with oil drops —retains the body heat. Somewhat belying its name, blubber is not soft and 'blubbery', but quite compact and firm.

Whales are divided into two distinct groups— the whalebone or baleen whales (*Mysticeti*) and the toothed whales (*Odontoceti*). The whale-whales have huge mouths with no teeth. Instead, sheets of whalebone or baleen attached to the gum of the upper jaws hang down vertically and are used to filter the large numbers of small animals, which are unselectively gathered. The toothed whales, on the other hand, do have teeth and so catch and devour individual prey animals in the same way as a terrestrial carnivore, such as a lion or tiger, feeds on land.

The whalebone whales are the most ancient of all the whales. Originating in the Cretaceous era about 100 million years ago, fossil specimens have been found, but they range in size from 3-17 m (10-55 ft) compared with 10-33 m (32-110 ft) of today's species. They are quite distinct from the toothed whales (which include the Sperm Whale and dolphins described in the next chapter) and the now extinct group known as the Archaeoceti or Zeuglodont whales. The Archaeoceti included a snake-like species, *Archaeocetes*, that lived during the Eocene, and must surely have been the nearest animal to resemble the mythological sea serpent that has ever existed.

The most modified of the ten species of whalebone whales are the Biscayan and Greenland Right Whales (*Balaena glacialis* and *Balaena mysticetus*). They were called Right Whales by the early whalers, for they were not only slow swimmers and easy to catch, but when they were killed, unlike most other whales, they floated, instead of sinking. They were therefore quite definitely the 'right' whales to catch. It is interesting to note that in one of the whalebone whales, the Fin Whale, the embryos develop tooth buds, thereby portraying ancestral links with a normally toothed mammal type. The teeth do not develop however, but disappear before the calf is born, to be replaced by the baleen plates. The inner edges of these are frayed into hairy fringes which form a massive filter. In the Biscayan Right Whale the longest of the 230 pairs of black baleen plates measures some 3 m (10 ft), whereas in the Greenland Right Whale or Bowhead Whale there are 300 pairs of black baleen plates, the longest of which is over 4 m (13 ft 4 in). To accommodate these long curtains of plates the upper jaw or rostrum of the Greenland Right Whale is arched up, (which is how it came by its alternative name of Bowhead Whale), and a third of its 20 m (65 ft) body length is taken up by its extraordinary head. These whales swim

BELOW LEFT A Blue Whale (*Balaenoptera musculus*) blowing at the surface. This, the largest mammal ever to live on Earth, has been reduced to dangerously low numbers by over exploitation.

BELOW A Grey Whale (*Eschrichtius gibbosus*) cow, accompanied by a calf, surges through the waves. Its grey colour, with the irregular white mottling, explains its colloquial name.

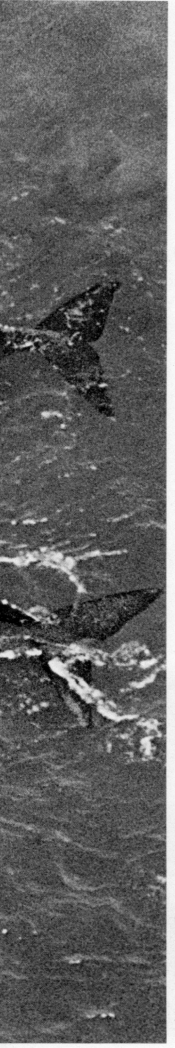

LEFT In the San Jose Gulf off Patagonia, a group of Southern Right Whales (*Balaena australis*) enter into a mating chase, close inshore. These whales are now completely protected.

RIGHT A Grey Whale (*Eschrichtius gibbosus*) sounds, lifting its tail flukes high above the sea surface. At times of danger, the flukes are crashed back down into the water as a warning signal.

BELOW As a Finback Whale (*Balaenoptera physalus*) is flensed at the Durban Whaling Station, the baleen plates which it uses to sieve plankton from the water, are uncovered.

slowly along with their mouths open, sieving huge numbers of small shrimp-like euphausiids from the water. Bowheads are confined to Arctic Waters from Alaska to Greenland in sea water temperatures of 0.5°C, (33°F) and are usually found close to the Arctic pack ice. They were exploited by British and Dutch whalers off Spitzbergen in the early 17th century, and the practice continued on through the 18th and 19th centuries, with the Eskimos also catching a few. Not surprisingly, this has led to a great scarcity of these slow, ponderous animals, although under the complete protection now afforded them, they are gradually increasing in numbers again.

The Biscayan Right Whale lives in more temperate waters, and was the first whale to be exploited by the Basques in the 16th century. An entirely separate population exists in the southern hemisphere, where it is known as the Southern Right Whale. Both populations move into higher latitudes during the summer months, but they do not inter-mix. This fat whale shows a large pro-

portion of its body above the water and when diving it always displays its tail flukes. The top of the snout is often discoloured with a great collection of parasitic growths.

At sea, the right whales can be distinguished from all the other whales, except for the Grey Whale (*Eschrichtius gibbosus*) by their V-shaped blow. The blow-hole of all whalebone whales is on the top of the head, roughly above the eyes, and it is this part of the whale that is clear of the water as it lies resting at the surface. As it exhales, a plume of condensation and steam spurts from the twin openings of the blow-hole. The twin plumes of the Right Whale's blows are 3-4m (10-13ft) high, while in the Grey Whale's it is 3m (10ft) high and may be either single or double. In all the other whalebone whales, it is single and vertical.

The Grey Whale occurs only in the North Pacific. It grows to about 15m (45ft) long and is grey coloured with irregular white mottled markings. On the underside of its throat there are two to four short furrows or grooves. The rostrum is only

slightly arched as its baleen plates are barely 0.5 m (1 ft 8 in) long. During the summer it feeds in the far north in the Bering and Okhotsk Seas on euphausiids and amphipods, relatives of the beach sandhoppers, which it is reputed to stir up from the sea bed with its snout. In autumn one population migrates down to the southern tip of Korea, while the other goes down to South California, to breed in shallow bays and lagoons. This habit made the Grey Whale particularly vulnerable to exploitation and at one time they were nearly exterminated. Since 1938, when they were given complete protection, the Californian Grey Whale population has recovered considerably and is now over 10,000 strong. Its playful antics in the surf has made it a great tourist attraction as it journeys down the west coast of the States on its way to the breeding ground in Southern California.

Fossil remains of Grey Whales have been found in Europe and North-west Africa and it is thought possible that this was the first whale population ever to be exterminated by stone-age man. This is only a theory, however and not one substantiated by evidence from cave paintings which one might expect to find. The earlier whalers working off the Aleutians called the Grey Whale, 'devil fish' or 'hardheads' because of the ferocity of their attacks on small whale boats when harpooned. The Grey Whales normally idle along at 1½-3 knots, but on their migration trips they travel at 6 knots. If pursued in earnest, they can keep up a speed of 9-10 knots for a short while. This is faster than a Right Whale's top speed of 5 knots, similar to the speed of Humpback Whales, and much slower than the speed of three other large species of whalebone whales.

Humpback Whales (*Megaptera novaeangliae*) occur in all oceans in water temperatures ranging from 0-30°C (32-86°F). They have very long narrow flippers which can be as much as one third of their total 17 m (50 ft) body length, and which they wave as they make their spectacular jumps right out of the water. On the underside of the body, eighteen to twenty-six grooves extend back as far as their navel. The overall grey-black colour, which is darker on the under surface, is often discoloured with parasitic whale lice and barnacles on the head and flippers.

Humpbacks feed mainly off planktonic crustaceans such as euphausiids, as well as squid and some fish. Like the majority of the other whalebone whales, they feed at high latitudes during the summer months and migrate southwards into warmer tropical and subtropical waters during the winter when the 4.2 m (14 ft) calves are born. The Humpbacks migrate close in along coast lines and so it has been possible to thoroughly study the pattern and timing of their migration. Some unaccounted oddities were found to occur in some of the migrations; for example, Humpbacks migrate northwards up the east coast of New Zealand, but return southwards down the west coast. Northern and southern hemispheres populations are separated in both time and space, for when the northern hemisphere populations are in tropical waters, it is summer and the feeding season in the south. Even the southern group is separated into different populations which breed on grounds at low altitudes inshore on each side of South America, Africa and Australia and also south of Fiji and the Pitcairn Islands. Each of these populations tend to exploit differing sectors of the Antarctic Ocean as feeding grounds. Some interchange between stocks has been shown to occur by whale marking, but it is limited. After heavy exploitation had reduced the stock of Humpbacks in the Weddell Sea area, replacement by individuals from other sectors took place very slowly.

There is a definite order in the pattern of migrations. The first whales to migrate north are the females nearing the end of lactation with calves they are weaning. They are followed by the immature males and females, then the mature males and the resting females, and finally the females in late pregnancy. Whales that have been taken in tropical waters always have empty stomachs, so it appears they starve during the several months they spend at low latitudes, living off the food reserves laid

ABOVE LEFT Seen head-on underwater a Grey Whale (*Eschrichtius gibbosus*) is an imposing sight. All over its head are growths of barnacles that are able to settle on these relatively slow swimming whales.

ABOVE Humpback Whales (*Megaptera novaeangliae*) are one of the whale species that frequently lift their tail flukes clear of the water as they sound.

RIGHT A Grey Whale (*Eschrichtius gibbosus*) rears its head up out of the water, showing its heavy infestation of barnacles and its mottled grey and white colouration.

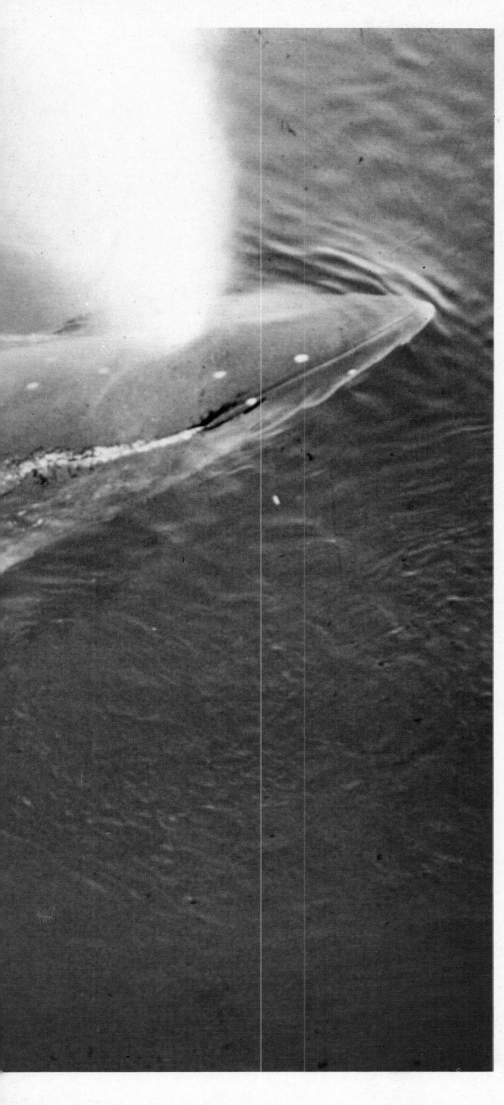

down during the summer months. The animals that probably need more food than average are the pregnant females that are the last to leave the feeding grounds. Similarly, the first to return south are the early pregnant females, then come the resting females and the males. Last to return are the females with newly born calves, so the calves, which have a thinner insulation of blubber, spend about two months less in the cold Antarctic waters than most of the adults.

The faithfulness with which the Rorqual Whales (genus *Balaenoptera*, including the Fin, Blue and Sei whales) return to the home feeding grounds is illustrated by the recovery of seven whale marks in 1952 from whales originally tagged in the same area between 1935 and 1938. The most successful whale marks are those devised by the Discovery Committee, and comprise a tube over 20cm (8in) long made of stainless steel. The mark is fired by a harpoon gun into the whale at a range of 20m (65ft) and is recovered only when a marked whale is captured, usually by retrieving it from the bottom of the blubber cookers. The marks are extremely useful in determining such things as how long whales live and at what age they become sexually mature. They also indicate the rate of exploitation; between 1949 and 1962, for example, the Japanese marked forty eight Blue, 685 Fin, 233 Sei and Bryde's and 343 Humpback Whales for which the recoveries were ten, 119, thirty-nine and six respectively.

As previously mentioned, populations of many species of whales have been seriously depleted, almost to the point of extinction in some cases, through man's whaling activities. The Humpback Whales, in the Antarctic in particular, were quickly reduced by such activities to extremely low population levels, after which the main objective of the whaling fleets in this region, became the Rorqual Whales. These faster swimming whales could only be caught by using fast-moving whaling boats capable of steaming at 15-20 knots, and also only after a Norwegian called Svend Foyn invented the explosive harpoon head in 1868. As these whales sink when killed, compressed air is used to make them buoyant. Blue and Fin Whales (*Balaenoptera physalus*) cruise at 10-12 knots and can speed at 18-20 knots for up to quarter of an hour, although it is reported that Fin Whales (which reach a maximum length of about 28m (88.5ft) weighing approximately 97 tonnes), can achieve speeds of more than 30 knots over short distances underwater. Sei Whales (*Balaenoptera borealis*), which are smaller, are probably even faster. All rorquals tend to have simple vertical blows, which are distinguishable only by experienced observers. In contrast to the Humpback Whales they rarely expose their flukes when sounding.

The main source of food for the Baleen Whales in Antarctic waters is the krill (*Euphausia superba*). This shrimp-like crustacean grows up to 5 cm (2 in) in length and swarms in enormous shoals in the region of the Antarctic convergence in the southern summer. This is the circumpolar region where the sea water, cooled and diluted by the melting ice, encounters the warmer, saltier water from further north. The environmental conditions favour tremendous growth by the microscopic plants, which in turn are fed on by the krill. Immense swarms of krill tend to form near the surface, often discolouring the water, and the biggest swarms seem to occur in the current eddies that develop to the lee east of the island arcs, to the south and east of Cape Horn. Antarctic Penguins, Crab-eater Seals and some fish, also feed on krill.

The main whaling grounds used to be in the vicinity of South Georgia and the South Sandwich Islands and it has been calculated that prior to 1930, at which time the Antarctic whaling industry really got under way, about 400,000 Humpbacks and Rorquals lived there. The whales themselves weighed about 25×10^9 kg, (equivalent to 25 million tonnes) and ate about three times this weight of krill during the feeding season, that is an estimated rate of 750,000 tonnes of krill a day.

It has been estimated that the filtering area of the baleen plates of a Blue Whale is 4.6 sq m (152.3 sq ft) and that its mouth volume is 4.5-6 cu m (158.8-211.8 cu ft) so each time a Blue Whale takes a gulp of water, it filters about 5 tonnes. The stomach contents of one whale were found to weigh 425 kg (936 lb). No wonder they school in areas where the biggest swarms of plankton occur! The reduction in the stocks of whales in the Antarctic has correspondingly led to vast swarms of krill being available for other krill-eaters and within the last decade there have been population explosions amongst such species as the Crab-eater Seal and some of the penguins. The increased populations of these competitive species means that the recovery of the whales may be slowed, even if all whaling is totally abandoned. However, the increase in the abundance of the food available to the few whales remaining, has resulted in their much faster growth, and as they have become sexually mature at the age of five years instead of ten to fifteen years, there is also an increase in the frequency of pregnancy.

ABOVE A Blue Whale (*Balaenoptera musculus*) hauled up onto the plan deck of a whale factory ship, dwarfs the men standing round. The throat grooves are clearly illustrated in this photograph.

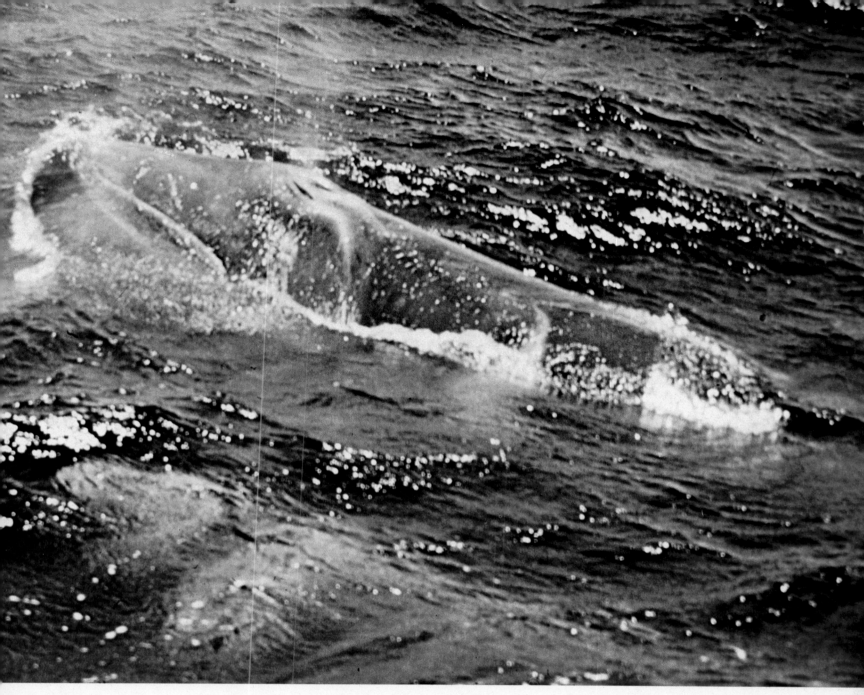

ABOVE A pair of Sei
Whales (*Balaenoptera
borealis*) at the surface.
One clearly shows the
twin blow-holes that are
typical of the whalebone
whales. The blow coalesces
into a single plume.

At the time of fertilization, the egg of a Blue Whale weighs less than a milligramme. During the fifteen to sixteen month gestation period, it grows to produce a calf, which, at birth, is 6.5-8.5 m (20-27 ft) long and which weighs about 3 tonnes. The calf is suckled for a year at the end of which time, it has increased its weight nearly nine-fold, weighing approximately 26 tonnes. At one time when the calf was weaned, the cows would have a further year of rest, but now they come into mating condition as they wean their calves. A male Blue Whale reaches maturity when he is about 22.56 m (74 ft) and a female when she is 23.46 m (77 ft). Both the size and the slaty-blue colour, make Blue Whales distinct from all other whales, although it would be rare indeed to find a 33 m (100 ft) long specimen in existence today. The throat of a Blue Whale has 70-118 grooves which extend back beyond the navel and the 7-12.5 m (23-41 ft) long baleen plates, including the fringe, are black.

The Blue Whales have a common name of Sulphur Bottom Whales, from the film of microscopic plants called diatoms that tend to develop on their undersides. The growth of this film is associated with their migration to warm waters.

Although Blue Whales had been subjected to heavy exploitation for sometime, the Japanese did not extend their whaling activities to the Indian Ocean sector of the Antarctic until the late 1950s. Then, north of the Antarctic convergence in the waters round the Kerguelen, Marion and Crozet Islands, they found a stock of smaller Blue Whales. These were distinguishable from the ordinary Blue Whale in having fewer ventral grooves under the head, fewer baleen plates, different types of parasites, and the females matured at a size of 19 m (62 ft) instead of 23-24 m (75-78 ft). Named Pygmy Blue Whales, they are considered to be only a different subspecies, although the fact that new populations and subspecies come to light in this way, serves to illustrate how difficult it is to study these huge mammals in the vastness of the oceans. These Pygmy Blue Whales feed north of the Antarctic convergence on a smaller species of krill, called *Euphausia vallentini*.

In the northern hemisphere, the Rorqual Whales show slight variations in their migration patterns and in their food preferences. Blue Whales in the North Atlantic feed in the Arctic, right at the edge of the pack ice and overwinter between the

Canaries and the Cape Verde Islands. The feed mostly on the euphausiid relatives of the Antarctic krill, *Meganyctiphanes norvegica* and *Thysanoessa inermis*. In the Pacific, the Blue Whales do not seem to migrate north of the Aleutian Island chain.

The Fin Whales, on the other hand, migrate up through the Bering Strait into the Bering Sea, although a big population stays feeding south of the Aleutians. Another population, now much reduced, moves into the East China Sea. Scientists find that they can separate the populations migrating up and down the east and west coasts of the Pacific, as well as those in the East China Sea, on the basis of body markings and their blood groups. In the North Atlantic, the Fin Whales move up to the edge of the ice like the Blues, but over winter north of the Canary Islands. Together with the Humpbacks, they became known as Herring Whales to the Norwegians, because of their close association with the herring shoals and they often follow the vast shoals of capelin (a herring-like fish) that occur off Finnmark in the very north of Norway. At the same time other Fin Whales may be feeding off north-west Spain. The Fin Whales eat mostly euphausiids although they will also feed on fish and squid.

The Sei Whales do not migrate so far north in either the Atlantic or the Pacific, as the other rorquals. In the Atlantic, they rarely penetrate further north then 72°N, but they overwinter in much the same area as the Blue Whales, that is between the Canaries and the Cape Verde Islands. Sei Whales have much finer hairs on their baleen plates and as a result, feed on much smaller planktonic animals. In the North Atlantic their favourite food is the copepod *Calanus finmarchicus* which is only about 3mm (0.1in) long. The Sei Whales got their name from their close association with the shoals of Saithe, a fish of the cod family that also eats *Calanus*. In the North Pacific, however, the Sei Whales eat a small pelagic shrimp *Sergestes*, while off New Zealand and the Falkland Islands, they mainly consume the lobster krill—*Munida*—a

ABOVE On a flat calm day, a Minke Whale (*Balaenoptera acutrostrata*) is seen clearly showing its dorsal fin. Like many of the whalebone whales, Minkes penetrate well into polar seas during the summer months.

RIGHT Trapped within the pack ice a Lesser Rorqual or Minke Whale (*Balaenoptera acutrostrata*) struggles to keep open a blow-hole in the ice. This whale is doomed.

little pelagic squat lobster that occurs in massive swarms in these waters.

Sei Whales grow up to 20 m (63 ft) long, and, unlike the Blue Whales, their ventral grooves do not extend as far back as the navel. Their chin, throat and belly as far back as the anus is white, whereas in the Bryde's Whale it is darkly coloured, in the Blue Whale it is blue, and in the Fin Whale, the right side of the head is dark and the whole of the underside white. Sei Whales frequent coastal shipping routes, making them a common sight for sailors and other ocean travellers.

Bryde's Whale (*Balaenoptera edeni*) is widespread throughout the tropics and subtropics and is often confused with the Sei Whale. The two are distinguishable by the Bryde's Whale's longer ventral grooves, and the ridges that occur on the snout in some of its population. It also has coarse grey bristles on its baleen plates, which contrast with finer white hairs on the Sei Whale. However, as all these features can be examined only after capture, the two species are indistinguishable in the open ocean. Bryde's Whale is confined to warm waters of temperatures around 15-30°C (59-86°F), where it feeds mostly on shoals of pilchards, anchovies and other fish, although in Japanese waters it also eats euphausiids. Bryde's Whale becomes sexually mature at the relatively small length of 12 m (36 ft), but it is also known to grow up to 15 m (50 ft).

Another small Rorqual Whale is the little Piked or Minke Whale (*Balaenoptera acutrostrata*), which has similar distributions to those of the Blue and Fin Whale, although it is now probably the most abundant whale in the Antarctic. The name 'Minke' is derived from the name of a member of Svend Foyn's crew (the inventor of the explosive harpoon) called Meincke, who made the 'beginner's' mistake of thinking a school of these little 10 m (30 ft) whales were Blue Whales. Like Bryde's Whale, however, they are more fish eaters than plankton feeders, and in consequence, the baleen plates of the Minke, although numbering about 300, are only 20 cm (8 in) long. This compares with 36 cm (14.5 in) in the Bryde's Whale and 60 cm (2 ft) in the Sei Whale. Minke Whales have fifty to seventy grooves extending half way back to its flippers, which have a white patch on the outer surface. Although its small size has meant it has never been exploited commercially for its oil, it has made it a useful source of meat, being quick to butcher and get into the deep freeze! The meat is also reputed to be excellent eating. The Norwegians began to exploit the stocks of Minkes off their coast during and just after World War II and by 1949 when protective measures were taken, some 4000 had been caught.

During the summer, Minke Whales penetrate far into high latitudes and those whales which are late to leave the polar seas sometimes become cut off from the open sea by pack ice forming round them. They survive for a time but presumably die when the

winter blizzards finally freeze over their blow-holes.

As in the other rorquals the sexes segregate during their migration. They are immensely curious whales and in 1963 while scientists on RRS 'Discovery' were working water bottles in the Indian Ocean, they were watched for half an hour by a pair of Minkes. The whales remained throughout with their heads clear of the water, watching every move the scientists made. Minkes share with Humpbacks the habit of leaping almost completely clear of the surface at times, and they are also quite sociable, forming schools of up to a hundred, which are probably maintained by calls.

Whales are extremely vocal animals, and although the whalebone whales do not seem to have developed the use of sound for echo-location as have the toothed whales, they nevertheless do use sounds for communication. Records of the calls of Humpback and Grey Whales have actually become best selling nature recordings. Whales have no outer lobes to their ears, (another adaptation to the general stream-lining of their body), but these have a curious internal structure. Experts disagree whether whales hear sound in the water, through their blubber and flesh, or whether it has to be conducted down through the plug of wax that seals the outer ear—a necessary feature to stop the ear flooding with water when the whale dives. As a whale grows, so the wax plug in the ear has to be enlarged and since growth is related to the feeding season, the ear plug is enlarged intermittently. This appears to result in a laminar structure that is akin to the annular rings in a tree trunk, and these laminations are a valuable aid in assessing the age of rorqual whales. Other techniques used to tell the age are counting the ridges on the baleen plates, and sectioning of the female ovaries to count the number of corpora albicantia—scar-like marks that indicate the number of ovulations the cow has undergone. Unlike most mammals, the scars persist in whales, although they do not indicate that pregnancy necessarily followed the ovulation.

Whales are not only highly adapted to their aquatic habitat in their body shape, by the loss of the hind pair of limbs, the development of the horizontal flukes, general streamlining and loss of hair, but also in their physiology. For example, the whalebone whales are capable of staying underwater for up to an hour, which is five to fifteen times as long as any terrestrial mammals would be able to remain submerged. They are good, although not particularly deep divers, but as their food of planktonic crustaceans or small densely shoaling fish usually occur within the surface 200 m (650 ft), they have little need to dive deeper. Indeed, pressure tubes mounted on harpoons used by whalers show that even when

sounding to escape attack, whalebone whales dive only to about twice this depth.

Before whales dive, they inhale, as opposed to those other marine mammals, the seals, which exhale before diving. Their rigid rib cage protects the lungs from the hydrostatic pressure, which increases by one atmosphere (i.e. the normal pressure of the air at the surface of the sea) for every additional 10 m (30 ft) the whale submerges, and the walls of the bronchial tubes are reinforced with cartilaginous rings and spirals along their entire length, extending as far as the alveolar sacs. The importance of the lungs is two-fold; firstly, they supply oxygen to the blood and secondly, they remove the waste carbon dioxide produced by respiration. Since the exchange of gases occurs in the alveoli, it is important that these sacs continue to contain gas, and this is probably the function of the sphincter valves that occur in the walls of the ducts to the alveoli. In dolphins, there are also valves in the branchioles, but the more elaborate system is associated with the dolphins' repeated shallow diving rather than the deeper and more prolonged dives of the rorquals.

When a whale dives, it carries about forty per cent of its oxygen within its tissues, forty per cent in its muscles, and the remainder equally distributed between the blood and the gases in its lungs. In contrast a human diving carries twelve per cent in his tissues, thirteen per cent in his muscles, thirty-four per cent in his lungs and forty-one per cent in his blood. The whales are able to carry so much extra oxygen within their body tissues and muscles because these organs have about eight times the respiratory pigment, myoglobin, normal in terrestrial animals. Myoglobin forms a loose combination with oxygen and so acts as a store. It is the high myoglobin content that gives whale meat its dark colour.

A whale's heart beats relatively slowly, partly because of its great size. A Blue Whale's heart is about 2 m (6 ft 8 in) across and weighs more than 0.5 tonnes. In an idling Blue Whale, the heart probably beats at a rate of five to ten beats per minute. As a dolphin dives, its heart beat rate gradually slows, and this probably happens as rorquals dive too. A feature of the circulatory system in whales is the large area of retia mirabilia —spongy tissue which contains a system of fine branching arteries and veins, acting as blood reservoirs. These can be quickly filled or emptied, so as to regulate the blood pressure during rapid dives or surfaces. There are also two routes by which the brain can be supplied with blood. If, for example, a 30 m (100 ft) whale dives vertically, the pressure differences between its head and tail would be three atmospheres which, without such special adaptations, would completely upset the

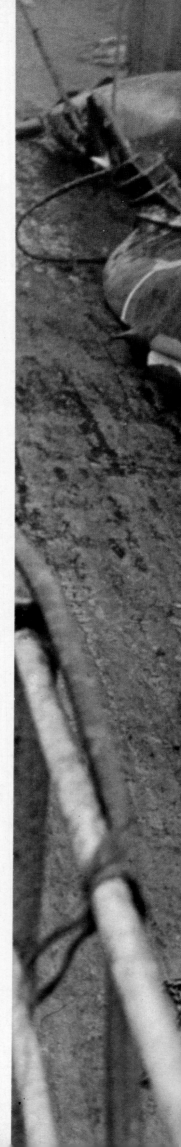

whole circulatory system. Furthermore, as it re-surfaces it has to breathe repeatedly to replenish its oxygen debt. As a whale swims underwater, a build-up of lactic acid occurs in the muscles and in the blood stream. Its production is the first step in breaking down carbohydrates in respiration, as it releases some of the energy stored in the carbohydrates but does not need oxygen. On surfacing, part of the lactic acid is completely broken down and part reconverted into carbohydrate—both processes needing oxygen. In the same way that a man who has sprinted 30 m (100 ft) continues to pant after the race, a whale has to repeatedly vent its lungs and increase its heart rate. Each blow by a large rorqual expels 1500 litres of air and reinflates the lungs in about two seconds, whereas the reader is probably breathing in and out 0.5 litres of air once every four seconds. The violence of these exhalations and inhalations would also cause violent pressure fluctuations in the blood supply without the dampening effect of the retia mirabilia.

A further interesting adaptation to the blood supply is in the arrangement of the vessels arriving at and leaving the tail flukes and flippers, the only parts of a whale not heavily insulated with blubber. The main functions of the blubber are to act as a food reserve and perhaps more importantly, to act as an insulation against heat loss. A whale maintains a body temperature of 35-36°C (95-97°F)—a degree or so lower than most other mammals. A full sized Blue Whale has a surface area of approaching 200 sq m (239 sq yds), so it has plenty of surface through which it can loose heat. It lives in an environment where the water temperature may range from a degree or so below zero to about 25°C (77°F), so it always requires adequate insulation, and especially so in the cold polar seas. The blubber provides such an effective insulation that a dead beached whale only cools off 0.1°C (0.18°F) in 24 hours. This explains why it decomposes so rapidly, generating a potent stench.

When a warm-blooded animal lives in a cold environment, there is an advantage in being large, because the surface area increases in proportion to the square of the body length; whereas the volume increases in proportion to its cube. Thus in a larger animal, the ratio between its body surface area and its volume is reduced and so the problem of maintaining the internal body temperature is also reduced. On land, there is a limit to the maximum volume of an animal, because as its volume increases, so its weight would increase and its legs would need to be correspondingly more massive to support it. Hence an elephant has heavy powerful feet, just so it can carry its own weight. In water, the weight problem is avoided and the limitation becomes the ability of the animal to catch enough food to sustain its bulk. If a Blue Whale doubled its length, the size of its filtering area would increase only by a factor of four, whereas its body volume would increase eight-fold. A full grown Blue Whale probably comes close to the maximum size a living animal could ever actually attain.

It has been calculated that if a whale just lay passively in the water, it would need a layer of blubber 13 cm (5 in) thick to stop it cooling down. In fact, whales seldom have this thickness of blubber because they are almost continually active, although there are reports of their sleeping. If a human runs around, he gets hot, and so will a whale if it is highly active. With too much insulation, it might suffer severely from over-heating and in fact, a beached whale quickly dies because it overheats. Thus elaborate precautions have to be taken to keep a whale cool when transporting it to a dolphinarium.

After a vigorous dive a whale needs to loose the heat it has gained. A man will sweat after excessive exertion, and as the sweat evaporates from his skin surface, it cools the skin. Sweating would be of no value to a whale immersed in water and indeed they have no sweat glands, so instead, they substantially increase the blood flow to their fins and flukes. A polar explorer, experiencing a feeling of overheating in his highly insulated clothing, can lose enough heat through one hand to compensate by merely removing one glove. Once he has cooled down sufficiently, he will replace his glove. Similarly, once sufficiently cool, a whale redresses the balance by reducing the flow of blood again to the uninsulated parts of its body. It also has a system of blood vessels leading to the fins and flukes where the veins run close alongside the arteries. These effect a heat exchange system whereby the warm arterial blood heats up the returning venous blood. The cooled arterial blood then has less heat to lose to the surrounding water, while the venous blood is almost warmed back up to the general body temperature.

It seems likely that the extensive migrations that many of the whales undergo are related to their need to conserve heat and energy in the winter months, when feeding is impossible at high latitudes. By moving into warmer low latitude waters, whales lose heat more slowly and therefore do not need to draw so much on their stores of energy. Even so, in the four to six months of starvation, a whale will use about half its reserves of blubber. In warmer waters survival of the calves, with their initially thin layer of blubber, is probably increased. Also the calf's demand for milk is reduced and so the suckling cow's blubber reserves will last longer.

Toothed Whales, Dolphins and Porpoises

Somewhat lesser in size, if not in potential menace —the toothed whales, which include the Sperm Whale or Cachalot (*Physeter catodon*) and the smaller whales and dolphins—are quite distinct from the whalebone whales discussed in the preceding chapter. It seems likely that they have been separate for at least forty million years, and besides differences in the general body organization of toothed whales, there are marked differences in the chemical composition of their fats and oil, in the structure of their blood proteins and of the myoglobin in their body tissues. They tend to be much smaller than the whalebone whales and all are carnivores feeding on fish or squid or large crustaceans. In general toothed whales eat approximately five per cent of their total body weight in food each day.

As toothed whales are much easier to capture, keep and train, considerably more is known about their behaviour and physiology, than the whalebone whales. However, as none of these, apart from the Sperm Whales at least, have been commercially exploited on a world-wide basis, our knowledge of many aspects of their natural history is considerably lacking. It was hard enough establishing the migration routes of Sperm Whales, but small shy species of dolphin which can be accurately identified only by thorough measurements of body proportions, can, and do, escape detection. It is hardly surprising, therefore, that new species are still being discovered, while three species of small toothed whales are known only from a single specimen. They are Longman's Beaked Whale (*Mesoplodon pacificus*), known only from a skull found on a beach in Queensland, Australia, in 1926; The New Zealand Beaked Whale (*Tasmacetus shepardi*) known from a single beached specimen found in 1937, and Hose's Sarawak Dolphin (*Lagenodelphin hosei*), known from a putrefying corpse found in the mouth of the Lutong River in Borneo in 1895.

The Sperm Whale is the largest of all the toothed whales. It has teeth only in its lower jaw and they fit into sockets in the upper jaw. The whale's huge blunt snout projects forwards far in front of the mouth below. Considerable discrepancy in size exists between the sexes. The bulls grow over 20 m (63 ft) long and tip the scale in the region of 75 tonnes, while the much smaller cows rarely exceed 12 m (39 ft) and weigh only about 16 tonnes. The sexes segregate during the summer, the bulls migrating far into high latitudes, whereas the cows stay in warmer seas. For example in the North Atlantic, the bulls were exploited off Iceland while the schools of cows stayed approximately in the vicinity of the Azores.

The distribution pattern of Sperm Whale movements was well documented in 1935, when data for nearly 37,000 Sperm Whales caught by American whalers between 1765-1920, were collected from the log book of the whaling captains kept in the New Bedford library. Sperm Whale hunting began in 1712 and within sixty years 125 ships were plying the world's oceans for these whales. Since Sperm Whales frequent tropical and sub-tropical waters and also deeper waters than the previously exploited species, a world-wide search had to be conducted to find the centres where they were concentrated. In 1789 the 'Amelia' left London and was the first sperm whaler to round Cape Horn into the Pacific. Catches were so good that by 1846 over 600 whalers were working out of Honolulu.

The cows and calves allowed themselves to be slaughtered passively, in fact the whalers would often kill the calf because the cow would stay near the body of her offspring and, in turn, be readily massacred. Similarly, attacking the cows was a sure way of keeping the bulls close by, handy for slaughter, for the bulls would stay near in order to try and help their wounded mates. The bulls, however, could be extremely dangerous, leaping clear of the water and lashing out with their huge flukes. Alternatively they would charge the boats and ram them head-on. Some of these ferocious bulls, such as Timor Tim, Don Miguel, Marquan, New Zealand Jack and Newfoundland Tom, became legends, all notorious for the ferocity of their attacks on whalers. The most famous of them all was Moby Dick, immortalized in Herman Melville's novel. Even today, reports of Sperm Whales attacking and ramming small crafts in the Pacific are not uncommon, although they are probably associated with the inter-bull fights when they compete for possession of the harem. To a distraught bull Sperm Whale, anxious to establish his territorial rights, a small boat, probably looks much like a rival!

The main value of the Sperm Whale was its oil and spermaceti—a whitish, semi-liquid substance

BELOW LEFT The head of a
Pacific Pilot Whale
(*Globiocephala scammoni*)
shows the peg-like teeth,
common to most toothed
whales, and the bulbous
development of its head.

BELOW A young Sperm
Whale calf (*Physeter
catodon*) lolls at the
surface, while the cow
feeds deep below. At birth
the calf was nearly 5 m
(16ft) long.

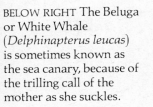

LEFT A White Whale (*Delphinapterus leucas*) in a dolphinarium begs for food. In the wild it will feed on a wide variety of shallow-living fishes.

RIGHT A pack of Sperm Whales (*Physeter catodon*) cruising off the coast of South Africa. Such groups may either be breeding females or a harem under the watchful eye of a bull.

BELOW RIGHT The Beluga or White Whale (*Delphinapterus leucas*) is sometimes known as the sea canary, because of the trilling call of the mother as she suckles.

FAR RIGHT A pair of Sperm Whales (*Physeter catodon*) making off at the approach of a ship. Activities of whalers have made these whales nervous towards ships.

obtained from the oil in the head. These were used for fuel and in the making of candles, ointments and cosmetics. From the middle of the 19th century the American Sperm Whaling Industry went into decline, not so much then, from the conservation pressures prevalent today, as from the effects of the manpower demands of land-based industry, the sinking of many whalers during the Civil War, and the discovery of mineral oil in Pennsylvania in 1859. Even so, it was not until 1925 that the last two whalers returned to New Bedford. Despite the many thousands of whales that were taken by the American whalers, extremely little of scientific value emerged from their exploitation. At the height of its prosperity the annual catch rate was about 10,000 whales, which is much the same as the estimated rate of exploitation that takes place currently.

The Sperm Whale is a remarkable animal in many ways. It is undoubtedly the deepest diving mammal; a medium sized bull was found entangled in a submarine cable at a depth of nearly 1200 m (3950 ft) off the north coast of Peru in 1955. An indication that they can dive even deeper, came from observations made from a spotter aircraft used for sighting the whales and calling in the whale catchers, homing on their quarry. Flying off Durban in 1969, a pair of isolated whales were spotted in an area where the sounding was well in excess of 2000 m (6560 ft) for a radius of over 48 kilometres (30 miles). The whales sounded. One surfaced fifty-three minutes later and the other after an hour and fifty-two minutes. When both whales were captured, two small black sharks, normally only to be found on the sea bed were found in the stomach of one.

Sperm Whales diving to these depths, would normally be pursuing their favourite food of squid, that frequent the ocean deeps. In fact, the main source for obtaining scientific specimens of these huge molluscs, some of which grow to a truly vast size, is from the freshly eaten specimens found inside whale stomachs. The heads of Sperm Whales and other squid-eating whales are often heavily scarred by the hooks on the arms of these squid, but since the eyes of the Sperm Whale are small and rather poor, it was always a puzzle to know how they located their prey.

It is clear that even the old whalers knew that Sperm Whales had an extremely acute sense of hearing, for they went to considerable lengths to muffle their oars and keep as silent as possible when stalking their prey. Observers from spotter aircraft have reported that even when the whale catchers are still 16 kilometres (10 miles) away, the behaviour of the whales will change. The bulls, especially, start to show their flukes and crash them down onto the waves, and immediately the whales in the vicinity begin to make off at speed. This fluke crashing behaviour appears to be a warning signal to the rest of the school, and explains the apparently aggressive behaviour of bulls as they lash out violently at nearby boats with their flukes.

As well as their acute hearing facilities, it also became apparent that Sperm Whales are extremely vocal and can produce a whole range of sounds—best described as squeaks, clicks, whistles and clucks. This is now known to be a characteristic feature of all the toothed whales and, for example, the Beluga or White Whale that abounds in the Arctic is known as a Sea Canary because of its trilling voice. This can be heard above water and appears to be often associated with the cow finishing suckling. Observations made on dolphins in captivity indicate that certain types of sound are used to communicate between the individuals in a school. Alarm calls, for instance, are usually short sharp whistles, and it is quite clear from the way in which dolphins will come to the assistance of wounded or endangered individuals that distress calls are transmitted quite long distances through

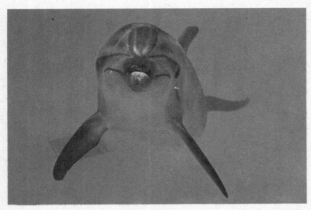

the water. However, the most interesting noises the toothed whales produce are the 'trains' of clicks. Individually these clicks vary in length from 0.1 milliseconds in some dolphins, to 25 seconds in Killer Whales. The frequency of the sound produced by Killer Whales is modulated during the click, so that trains of ten to fifteen clicks may be produced in some species changing from high to low frequency. In Sperm Whales the trains consist of six to nine pulses, each lasting 0.1-0.2 milliseconds, over a period of about 24 milliseconds. The timing and the variations in intensity of the train of pulses may act as a personal signature, so that a whale can distinguish the echoes of its own sound from the echoes of the clicks of its companions in the school.

The function of these clicks is to echo-locate food—a technique which is also used by flying bats to catch insects on the wing. Bats listen to the echoes of their own squeaks bounced back off their prey. Observations suggest that Sperm Whales can hear each other over distances of about 10 kilometres (6 miles) and that their echo-locating range is at least 1000 m (3280 ft). It would seem essential for an air breathing animal feeding on deep-living animals, to avoid abortive energy-consuming dives, by first locating (and, possibly even identifying) its prey before it dives. To achieve this the sound would need to be 'focused'

in some way. Dolphins appear to produce their clicks by extruding a fine stream of bubbles out of their blow-hole, possibly with the aid of the valves and associated little sacs. The shrieks they can produce seem to come from their larynx in much the same way that human speech is formed. The front of the dolphin's cranium has flat forward facing surfaces that act as a reflector of the sound, and the pad of fat overlying the skull on the front of the face acts as a sound 'lens', concentrating and directing the acoustic signal forward. If a dolphin is swimming straight towards a hydrophone, therefore, it will pick up the sounds loud and clear, but the intensity diminishes considerably as soon as the dolphin turns slightly to one side.

Scientists using echo-sounders to study fish in the sea find that low frequency sound (i.e. 10 kilohertz) travels further than high frequency sound (i.e. 200 kilohertz). High frequency sound gives much better discrimination of the size of the target than low frequency. Dolphins are sensitive to sound up to 200 kilohertz in frequency, whereas man's sensitivity ceases at around 20 kilohertz. The variations in frequency produced during a click, probably allows the dolphin initially to locate distant objects; then, as it approaches, it can begin to judge the size and numbers of the targets. Dolphins are quite capable of distinguishing between 15 and 30 cm (6 and 12 in) long fish. They can avoid wires of 2.8-4.0 mm (0.1-0.15 in) diameter and can be trained to choose between targets varying by only seven per cent in their cross-sectional area. They can discriminate between objects varying by 2-3 mm (0.07-0.11 in) in size in the horizontal plane and 3-5 mm (0.11-0.19 in) in the vertical plane.

The remarkable domed head of the Sperm Whale possibly has a similar function to that of the dolphin—that is, as a focusing device for its echo-locating system, but there has also been a suggestion that it relates to the buoyancy of the whale. A harpooned Sperm Whale sinks and so it is heavier than water. At its blood temperature,

LEFT Sperm Whales (*Physeter catodon*) hardly break the surface as they blow, and so may be difficult to spot. The small dorsal fin is set well back down the body.

BELOW Disorientated by the echoes in a shallow bay at Cape Schanck, Australia, this school of Sperm Whales (*Physeter catodon*) were stranded and died of overheating.

the whale's spermaceti is in a transition phase between being solid and liquid; when it solidifies, it is heavier than when it liquifies. Thus calculations suggest that if all the spermaceti is liquid, the whale will become slightly buoyant, so, if during a dive, a whale warms up its spermaceti, its return to the surface will be easier. The Sperm Whale is also exceptional in having its blow hole on the front edge of its head which suggests that on its return to the surface the head is anyway slightly cocked up by its buoyancy. The 6m (19ft 6in) long blow of a Sperm Whale is

immediately distinguishable from all other whales that produce visible blows, because it is directed obliquely forward. The blow-hole of all toothed whales is single, whereas in all the whalebone whales, as previously seen, it is double.

A curious consequence of the system of echo-location of toothed whales is that massed strandings occasionally occur. Individual whale-bone whales are sometimes stranded but these are usually injured or senile specimens that have been washed inshore. The strandings of toothed whales appear to be a sort of madness that

suddenly afflicts a school and if any of the individual whales are towed back out to sea, they invariably turn straight around and beach themselves again. The only suggested reason for such strandings is that in shallow water their echo-location can get confused and disorientated. Natives of a village in the Solomon Islands use this disorientation to their own advantage. They drive schools of dolphins up into a funnel-shaped bay by clapping coconut shells together under-water. As the water gets shallower, the ring of canoes gets tighter, and the noise of the coconuts gets more intense until suddenly the dolphins bury their heads in the sea bed as they try to sound. The water is so shallow, their flukes are left beating in the air, and all the natives need to do is wade in and pull them on to the shore. Pilot Whales have been exploited in the Faeroes for many years by driving them ashore, where they provide a welcome source of meat in these austere islands.

Groups of toothed whales also sometimes come ashore in large numbers for no obvious reason. In 1927, 150 Killer Whales beached themselves at Dornoch, Scotland, and 167 were also found stranded at Velenai in Ceylon. The inhabitants of La Paz, California, had much to put up with in 1954, when twenty-four Sperm Whales came ashore—the stench of the decomposing corpses was getting intolerable when another school of thirty-four beached themselves fourteen days later!

The Sperm Whale's brain is the largest known in any animal; a 15 m (45 ft) male was found to have a brain weighing 8.5 kg (19 lb). This, however, is only 1/5000 of the body weight, and very small in comparison to the ratio of 1:60 in man. Anatomists, who have examined the brains of Sperm Whales, point out that the lobes of the brain concerned with sound reception are enormously well developed, whereas those associated with taste and smell are reduced. From this, they concluded that taste and smell were unimportant in the whale's life style.

The general difficulties of observing toothed whales in their natural habitats and the fact that some whales release a fright chemical into the

water, reduce the chances of proving the significance of taste and smell. A school of dolphins, being observed in shallow waters appeared to be suddenly frightened and made off into the open ocean; an hour later another school moving along the coast suddenly took evasive action at the same point, although nothing was seen to scare them. It is also thought that 'attraction' chemicals may be released, especially by cows ready for mating. Lone bull Sperm Whales have been seen to suddenly change course to follow the path of a school of cows, which had moved through the area several hours previously and were well out of ear-shot.

Dermal sensitivity to touch is also important. Captured dolphins can be quietened by stroking, while nudging and brushing alongside are important parts of love-play and pre-suckling behaviour in whales.

Reproduction in whales follows the normal mammalian pattern, except that it is highly modified for their aquatic life. Mating is performed in many species with the two animals positioned vertically in the water, and although copulation is relatively brief, lasting only a few seconds, the preceding love-play may last as much as half an hour. Gestation in the Sperm Whale

ABOVE Underwater, a Pilot Whale (*Globiocephala melaena*) quizzically watches the photographer.

RIGHT A Pilot Whale (*Globiocephala melaena*) blowing at the surface. These whales are called 'Blackfish' by fishermen.

BELOW An underwater view of a Pilot Whale (*Globiocephala melaena*) as it blows. The huge dome of its forehead is an adaptation to improve its echo-location of the fish schools, on which it feeds.

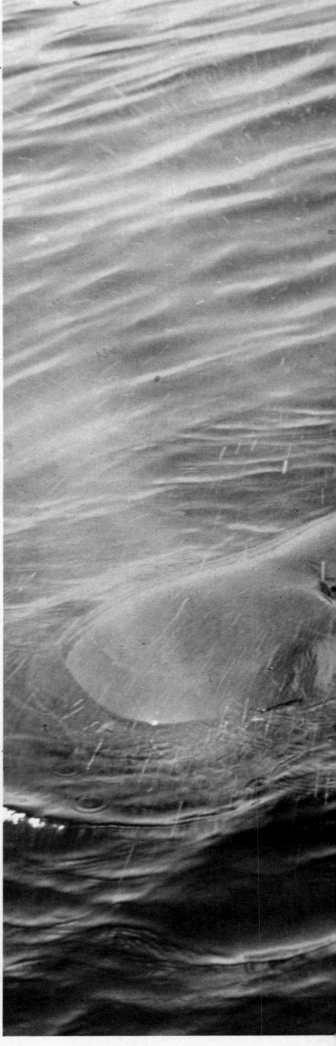

takes sixteen months, and a similar time in Pilot Whales. In dolphins it ranges from nine to twelve months, the smaller species having a shorter gestation than the larger ones. One curious fact about the developing foetus in some dolphins is that they temporarily develop up to eight nipples, so displaying their distant relationship to carnivores, such as dogs, otters and bears.

Multiple births in whales are extremely rare, probably because the calf needs to be well developed and able to swim independently, as soon as it is born. The calf is born tail first, in contrast to the usual head first presentation in other mammals and this probably helps to ensure that the newly born calf does not attempt to breathe until it is fully born and able to reach the surface. In the toothed whales, the calf at birth may be up to fifty-two per cent of the cow's length and ten to fifteen per cent of her weight. A newly-born Sperm Whale calf is about 4.27 m (14 ft) long and weighs about 1 tonne, compared with a fully mature cow's average length and weight of 11.58 m (38 ft) and 16 tonnes. It is interesting to note that, apart from whales, the only mammals to give birth underwater are sea cows and the hippopotamus.

The female whale's pair of nipples lie in slits far back on the underside of the belly; the nipple is extruded and the calf holds it between its tongue and palate. Suckling is induced by the calf nudging the belly of its mother and the milk is probably injected into the calf's mouth, but as the new-born calf can remain underwater for about half a minute, suckling lasts for only a few seconds. Initially a dolphin calf suckles every half hour, but after six months it suckles only seven or eight times a day and it is weaned after about a year. Sperm Whale and Pilot Whale calves are weaned nearly two years after birth.

As a Sperm Whale calf grows over 3.1 kg (7 lb) a day, the milk needs to be very nutritious. Its

ABOVE Dolphins (*Delphinus* sp.) are mammals and give birth to live young. Here in a dolphinarium is the moment of birth. In contrast to the normal mammalian pattern the calf is born tail first.

ABOVE RIGHT Dolphins (*Delphinus* sp.) gather into quite large schools of up to a hundred animals, like this group off New Zealand. The school hunts as a pack and cooperates in the defence of individual members.

RIGHT Many species of dolphin, like this Pacific Bottle-nosed Dolphin (*Tursiops truncatus*), love to sport riding the bow waves, just ahead of the bows of ships.

BELOW A close-up of the head of a Killer Whale (*Orcinus orca*) shows its impressive armament of peg-like teeth, and the characteristic black and white colouration.

RIGHT The first sign of the approach of a marauding pack of Killer Whales (*Orcinus orca*) may be recognized by the curving triangular fins cutting through the waves.

BELOW RIGHT Two Killer Whales (*Orcinus orca*) are seen desperately trying to keep their blow-holes open in the pack ice, as the icy grip of winter begins in Antarctica.

composition changes as the calf grows but generally it has the consistency of clotted cream, and it contains over a third fat. (An ordinary cow has an average of four per cent fat in her milk). The fat in Sperm Whale milk is more waxy than in other species, resembling spermaceti oil and the milk also contains about ten per cent of protein with a rather low content—only one to two per cent—of the sugar, lactose. A Sperm Whale's teeth do not erupt from the gums until the whale has become sexually mature.

The food of adult toothed whales varies between species. One of the axioms of zoology is that no two species can survive if they feed on precisely the same food, at the same place and at the same time. This is well illustrated by the two species of dolphins belonging to the genus *Stenella* which live in the same areas, but one feeds predominantly at depths of about 30m (100ft) and the other at 250m (820ft). A Bottle-nosed Dolphin needs to eat 5-15kg (11-33lb) of food a day, so the quantities of fish and squid consumed daily by the world's toothed whales has been estimated to reach a staggering 2 million tonnes. The type of food

taken varies seasonally and geographically. For example, in order of importance, the Beluga eats capelin, sand-eels, cod, bull-heads and flounders in the Gulf of St. Lawrence; in the White Sea it eats flounders, herring, capelin, sand-eels, cod and haddock; and off the north coast of the USSR, it eats northern cod, capelin, saffron cod, herring and sand-eels. Individuals may also show unusual tastes, and much of the notoriety of the Killer Whale is based on a finding of the remains of thirteen porpoises and fourteen seals in the stomach of a 7m (22ft) long specimen. Killers also earned the hatred of whalers because of the packs that would assemble to feed off the carcases of whale-bone whales waiting to be processed by factory ships. The more normal diet of the Killer Whale, however, includes fish, squid and the occasional shark as well as seals and birds. Even other small whales have been found in killer whales' stomachs.

In dolphinaria, Killer Whales have proved to be easily tamed and trained and even in the wild, there is one remarkable story of cooperation between Killer Whales and man, which took place in Twofold Bay, New South Wales. A pack of Killers

ABOVE The False Killer Whale (*Pseudorca crassidens*) is a totally black fish-eating dolphin, whose large triangular dorsal fin resembles that of a Killer Whale as it swims at the surface.

RIGHT A Killer Whale (*Orcinus orca*) and two Bottle-nosed Dolphins (*Tursiops truncatus*) in a dolphinarium, pose with their heads clear of the water, and so illustrate the differences between them in shape and colour.

BELOW A Beluga or White Whale (*Delphinapterus leucas*) photographed here in shallow water shows its blow-hole, paired flippers, dorsal fin and tail flukes.

BELOW CENTRE A stranded Narwhal (*Monodon monoceros*) bull shows the amazing length of its single tusk. These dolphins occur at high latitudes in the Arctic.

RIGHT A young Narwhal (*Monodon monoceros*) cruising at the surface shows that this curious animal is a type of dolphin. The tusk develops only in mature bulls.

used to drive whalebone whales into the Bay, where open boat whalers waited, to harpoon and kill the quarry. The corpse would sink to the bottom and the Killers would eat the tongue and lower jaw. After a couple of days the decomposing corpse floated to the surface, where the whalers collected it and towed it inshore for processing. This remarkable pack of Killer Whales was led by a bull Killer with an easily recognisable colour pattern, who was known as Old Tom. It is reported that he led his pack for ninety-two years, which makes him considerably older than the oldest Sperm Whale reported at sixty-five years, and the famous dolphin, Pelorus Jack. A great favourite among sailors, Pelorus Jack conducted ships through Cook Straits between the North and South Islands of New Zealand for thirty-two years.

As previously mentioned, Sperm Whales are famed for their diet of giant squid. A 14.6m (47ft) Sperm Whale taken off the Azores had a 10.49m (33ft) squid weighing 184kg (400lb) in its stomach, although generally, they feed on smaller specimens. That squid is a favourite meal among Sperm Whales is known by identifying the parrot-like squid beaks which accumulate in the whales' stomachs. These beaks are resistant to the digestive juices and seem to be passed slowly, if at all, through the whale's 400m (1310ft) intestine. It is the compaction of the beaks that is one suggested origin of the formation of ambergris. Ambergris is only found in the stomachs of a few Sperm Whales, but sometimes in huge lumps—the record being a lump weighing 455kg (902lb). It is rich in an aliphatic alcohol called ambrain and, with its musky odour and reputed aphrodisiac properties, it used to be in very high demand for the manu-

facture of perfumes. Maybe women would have had a different attitude to their allure, however, if they had only realized it depended on daubing extracts of none other than compacted Sperm Whale faeces on their bodies!

The battles that Sperm Whales have with their squid prey often leave them covered with scars— results of the wounds inflicted by the squid's hooked suckers. The wounds may take the form of long parallel scratches, or they may be circular in shape, in which case they can be up to 10cm (4in) in diameter. The Norwegian legend of the 'kraken' —a vast monster supposedly with 20m (60ft) long tentacles—probably originated from someone seeing a large bull Sperm Whale fighting with a giant squid. By moonlight, such a horrific sight would appear gigantic, and quite large enough to make credible the story that a bishop was able to

perform Mass on the back of a kraken! Reports that Sperm Whales aggregate into large schools near shallow banks during new and full moon nights, it is thought may be the result of the spawning behaviour of the squid.

Sperm Whales do not eat only squid; off Iceland, for example, they feed mostly on cod. Like the sharks discussed in Chapter 1, a medley of bizarre items have been found in the stomachs of Sperm Whales—rocks weighing 1.4kg (3lb), four litres of sand, a glass float, a cormorant, a shoe, plastic bags and baling wire, to mention just some!

Another whale that has given rise to a number of legends is the Narwhal—a curious whale, in which the male has a single, very long, spiral tusk. They are often attributed with being the source of the legend of the unicorn, and their tusk, when powdered down, was reputed to have miraculous

ABOVE Beaked Whales
are amongst the rarest of
all toothed whales. Here
an unidentified species of
Bottle-Nosed Whale
(*Berardius sp.*) surfaces and
shows its beak.

RIGHT Bottle-nosed
Dolphins (*Tursiops
truncatus*) are trained to
give entertainment in
dolphinaria. Here one
shows the row of peg-like
teeth in its lower jaw.

medicinal powers. It may be as long as 2m (6ft 8in) on a 4-5m (13-16ft) long animal, but it is very fragile and easily snapped, which perhaps explains why it is not used either in feeding or for defence. It is generally sighted as another example of the oddities thrown up by sexual selection, similar in concept to the massive antlers of the Irish Elk.

Narwals are actually a form of spotted dolphin, and are restricted to the Arctic north of 70°N. They come under attack from the Eskimos, who hunt them more for their skin than their meat. The skin is extremely rich in Vitamin C, containing as much as 31.8 milligrammes per gramme, and as this important dietary requirement is usually only found in fresh fruit and vegetables, such a source would be of great value to the inhabitants of the high Arctic. Like Belugas and Killer Whales, Narwhals sometimes form separate schools of male and females. It is said of them—and indeed of the Belugas from Greenland—that the tail of the foetus emerges four to six weeks before birth. The reason suggested for this, is that the foetus can practice swimming prior to birth!

There are several other extremely odd groups of small whales. The Beaked Whales of the genus *Mesoplodon*, for example, are mostly known only through stranded specimens. They have long jaws but only the odd tooth. Fossil species show that they have descended from ancestors that had many teeth, and so the classification of these toothless whales amongst the toothed whales is justified. Their loss of teeth appears to be an adaptation to squid eating. Six species of *Mesoplodon* occur in the North Atlantic, although only in restricted areas. The majority of the forty known strandings of Sowerby's Beaked Whales in the east Atlantic, have occurred on coasts round the North Sea; only three have been stranded on the east coast of North America. In contrast, eight specimens of True's Beaked Whale have been found along the North American eastern seaboard, and only four on the west coast of the British Isles.

There are two species of Pygmy Sperm Whales, which are almost as poorly known as the Beaked Whales. Although they are rare, they occur widely throughout the tropics and sub-tropics, where they appear to live in shallow water, feeding on crabs, shrimps and small squid. Much smaller than their close relatives, the Sperm Whale, they are only 2-3m (6-10ft) long and have very short heads. However, they have a spermaceti organ, a toothed assymmetrical lower jaw, and a single blowhole which is situated above the eyes instead of at the tip of the snout.

Favourite and best known of all the toothed whales, must be the dolphin. They will be familiar to visitors of marine parks and dolphinaria, as well as to anyone who has taken a long sea voyage and seen them sporting in the bow wave of ships, even when steaming at over 20 knots. Reliable measurements of swimming speeds suggest that dolphins can only maintain sprint speeds of 20 knots for one to two minutes. They maintain their speed in front of ships by riding the bow wave, hence appearing to have more stamina than in reality. Other toothed whales are also comparatively fast swimmers, even when not being hunted, and there is a reliable account of a school of Killer Whales about 6-7m (19-22ft) which approached a ship at an estimated 30 knots and continued to circle it for 20 minutes while it steamed along at over 20 knots. Although dolphins cannot claim the sea speed record for marine animals; this truly remarkable group of mammals undoubtedly win outright in the I.Q. stakes.

Naturally very playful, in captivity they readily settle down to life in a more restricted environment. They may be quickly trained to perform a whole range of acts, such as leaping through hoops, jumping vertically for fish, playing water polo, standing vertically out of the water, and to

temporarily beaching themselves. They are even said to practise these tricks on their own, when no trainer is present. The purpose of such training need not be just for entertainment but can also be used by scientists to assess the mammals' physiology. The record 6m (20ft) high jump by a Bottlenosed Dolphin called Pedro at the St Augustine Marineland in Florida, for example, can be used to estimate how fast a dolphin would need to swim to gain sufficient momentum to achieve such a leap.

Scientists were also able to assess how well a dolphin could see and differentiate between various colours, as well as the sorts of shape it could recognize, by training one to press a certain type of button for food. When it had learned to do this, it was given a choice of buttons and the alternatives were made progressively more and more similar to the correct button, which would reward the dolphin when it was pressed. The dolphin continued to press the correct button, until it was no longer able to distinguish it from the other buttons.

Besides the visual responses, it has also been possible to study the dolphin's ability to perceive sonically by fixing eyecups over the trained dolphin's eyes and running similar sorts of tests. They can also be trained to willingly carry instru-

ABOVE Pacific Bottlenosed Dolphins (*Tursiops truncatus*), viewed from above show their sleek streamlined shape. The scars were probably incurred during mating or inter-male rivalry.

ABOVE When whales idle along, the back just breaks the surface, but many when swimming at speed, leap well clear of the water. Dolphins, (*Delphinus* sp.) like this one, are particularly good jumpers.

ment packages, although it is probably just in the nature of a game to them. From these and other tests considerable information has been collected about their body temperatures and the composition and volumes of the air they exhale when they surface from a dive, and it has also been possible to follow their activity patterns even during hours of darkness. These measurements and assessments have been made on totally free swimming animals, as well as those in captivity.

The playfulness in dolphins, and indeed in other larger whales, probably has an important function in practising cooperation in schooling behaviour. An individual dolphin would be far less effective in surviving in the open ocean than a school which hunt together and cooperate in such practices as herding fish shoals. The school provides considerable protection to the young calves, as proved by the account in Chapter I of dolphins in a pool killing a shark by continually butting it. Although this probably would not happen in the wild, sharks would need to be particularly big and powerful, before they could confidently afford to brave the combined defence of a large school of dolphins. Dolphins have a remarkable record of assisting wounded or ill animals and will help their wounded mates up to the surface so that they

can continue to breathe. Newly born calves are often nudged to the surface to take their first breath by the mother and another dolphin acting as 'auntie' to the young animals.

Dolphins do not restrict their aid just to members of their own species. There are many accounts of their coming to the aid of other types of dolphins in Marinelands as well as to humans who find themselves in difficulty when swimming or shipwrecked. There is the famous tale from Greek mythology of a dolphin who rescued the musician, Arion, and took him safely to the shore, after he had been cast overboard by wicked sailors. A considerably more recent story, and one that is known to be true, is that of a Florida housewife who went out for an evening swim in 1949. She got into severe trouble and was on the point of drowning when she suddenly found herself supported in the water and pushed inshore to the beach. Uncomprehendingly, she got to her feet to be told by bystanders that she had been helped ashore by some dolphins. Perhaps if dolphins were terrestrial they would displace the dog as man's best friend, but then maybe with their ability to communicate and cooperate with one another, they might dominate the terrestrial environment usurping man as rulers of the world.

Sea Elephants and Sea Cows

Seals and sea lions must be among the best loved of all sea mammals and are known to visitors of zoos and circuses the world over. Their popularity can be judged by the violent reaction that has been evoked, not just by conservationists, but everyone, to the ruthless exploitation and seemingly unselective killing of vast numbers. They belong to a group of aquatic carnivores known as pinnipeds, while the unrelated large sea cows are termed sirenians.

The pinnipeds are divided into three sub-groups: the eared seals (Otariidae), the walruses (Odobenidae) and the true seals (Phocidae). All these animals have stream-lined, hairy bodies, four limbs modified as flippers, very short tails and a body-lining of blubber. The hind limbs are used like whale flukes, to propel them through the water. Some pinnipeds spend more time in water than they do on land, but they all leave the water to give birth, and usually to suckle their young. Births are single and the cows are generally impregnated soon after the birth of the pups, although implantation of the fertilized ovum may be delayed for three months or so. The growth of the foetus will start after the cow has completed suckling and has undergone a moult.

Despite the general similarities, anatomical and biochemical evidence suggests that the sub groups may not be derived from a common stock. The true seals seem most likely to have evolved from otter-like ancestors, while the eared seals, together with the walruses, are thought to have descended from bear-like animals, possibly along the Pacific coast of America, where the vast majority of their fossil remains have been found. However, the oldest pinniped fossils come from Miocene deposits laid down about 20 million years ago, and nearly all these may be easily attributed to one or other of the sub groups. The pinnipeds are a good example of convergent evolution; that is the tendency for animals colonizing a particular type of habitat to develop similar adaptations to life within that habitat, and so becoming more and more similar to each other.

Seals maintain an average internal body temperature of 36.5-37.5°C (97-99°F). Like whales, they have an immediate problem of how to maintain their internal temperature, and they have adopted several physiological solutions similar to those found in whales in order to cope with this. They have a thick body lining of blubber which certainly acts as insulation, and may also serve as a store for food reserves, as well as providing buoyancy in the water. In the Weddell Seal (*Leptonychotes weddelli*), for example, nearly a quarter of the average 450kg (992lb) of body weight, is blubber. Seals can reduce the blood circulation to the skin so as to conserve heat, and furthermore, similar to whales, the blood flowing through the uninsulated flippers passes through a counter-flow blood system that acts as a heat exchange. However, with the exception

BELOW LEFT A pair of heavily scarred and blood stained Northern Sea Elephants (*Mirounga angustirostris*) bulls fight over their territory on San Miguel island, California.

BELOW The hairless skin, and bristly muzzle, armed with a pair of ivory tusks, shows clearly in this head-on picture of a walrus (*Odobenus rosmarus*), as it surfaces in the sea off an Alaskan island.

of the Walrus (*Odobenus rosmarus*), pinnipeds have retained the normal mammalian covering of hair, in contrast to the whales. Groups of hairs grow out of individual follicles but emerge out of a single hair canal, and each group includes a single long coarse guard hair and a number of under fur hairs. In the Common or Harbour Seal (*Phola vitulina*), there are four to five under hairs, while the Northern Fur Seal (*Callorhinus ursinus*), has nineteen such hairs. This soft, under fur, acts as an underwater insulator by retaining a trapped layer of air during a dive. It also gives seal skins a very high commercial value.

Seals show interesting differences from whales in the way in which they dive. Whales take a deep breath before they dive, whereas seals exhale. The lungs are so designed that when a seal submerges, what little air remains, stays within the large trachea, which are supported by cartilaginous rings. An interesting exception is the Leopard Seal (*Hydrurga leptonyx*), whose trachea has cartilaginous bars allowing it to collapse when it swallows whole penguins down its gullet. As soon as a seal begins its dive, its heart beat rate slows right down. Although the blood supply to the general body organs is cut off, they nevertheless contain a considerable store of oxygen combined with the abundant myoglobin in the tissue. The blood supply to the brain is maintained,

using well oxygenated blood stored in retia— analagous to the way in which whales also store oxygenated blood. These adaptations, combined with the fact that the body tissues are able to tolerate high levels of dissolved carbon dioxide, mean that most seals can stay submerged for over half an hour. The deepest dive recorded by a seal was by a Weddell seal, which submerged for just over 43 minutes and reached a depth of 600 m (1968 ft). The animal had a depth gauge attached to it by American scientists who were engaged in work in McMurdo Sound.

Seals are amongst the faster swimming animals in the sea, although reliable speed records are few in number. Californian Sea Lions (*Zalophus californianus*) and Leopard Seals, are thought to be able to achieve speeds of over 32 km/h (20 mph) and the Northern Fur Seals, speeds of 27 km/h (17 mph). Californian Sea Lions in dolphinaria are capable of hurdling bars held above water and, when migrating in the open ocean, habitually 'dolphin'. A line of sea lions, all dolphining, resemble a sea-serpent. Nansen, the famous Norwegian Arctic explorer, also describes how during one of his journeys, a Hooded Seal (*Cystophora cristata*), leapt out of the sea, clearing a boat, to land on an ice floe which was 'the height of a man above the water'. This species of seal holds the seal marathon record;

ABOVE A female Weddell Seal (*Leptonychotes weddelli*) and her pup lie side by side on the snow. This seal is the most southerly of all the Antarctic species.

one was marked off Greenland and recaptured thirteen days later 640 kilometres (400 miles) away. On land, seals can also move quite fast; a Crabeater Seal (*Lobodon carcinophagus*), was able to keep ahead of a man running over level, hard-packed snow for over half an hour. The pursuer was physically fit and it was estimated that the seal was probably keeping up a speed of about 25 km/h (16 mph).

Seals have curious eyes. They are large and the cornea is flattened so that, in fact, they see better underwater than out of it. The iris of the Common (or Harbour) Seal is fully expanded and circular in water, whereas out of water, it closes down into a slit-like shape. Many seals contract the iris right down when subjected to air so that the eye focuses rather like a pinhole camera. When seals are hauled out of water, their fur is dry, but the area around the eyes, is wet with tears. The tear ducts are actually used to get rid of excess salt. Seals rarely get the chance to drink fresh water and will seldom drink it even when it is offered, but they do consume quite large quantities of salt water, both by drinking it and by inadvertently swallowing it with their food. Their blood salt concentration is about half that of sea-water. In most mammals the kidneys perform the function of regulating the salt level of the blood, but in seals, this is supplemented by the tear ducts, which excrete a concentrated

brine solution. Even in human beings, tears are appreciably salty.

On land, all male seals produce distinctly audible roars, grunts and barks, during their territorial fighting, or in response to disturbance by other animals, including man. Recently, underwater recordings show that several species of seal produce clicks and whistles, analagous to those used by toothed whales for echo-location. Certainly many seals feed nocturnally, and many feed in murky water, and so it would not be surprising to find that seals too, may have an echo-location ability. A blind Grey Seal (*Halichoerus grypus*) cow, studied in the Hebrides, was clearly able to feed and keep healthy. She gave birth to a pup, reared it successfully and was quite able to relocate it in a crowded rookery, just by her senses of touch, smell, and presumably, echo-location underwater.

Many species have very long whiskers, well supplied with sensory endings, which are used to taste and feel out food. They tend to be particularly well developed in bottom feeding species. The Walrus feeds on bivalve molluscs and has a most impressive moustache of about 400 whiskers. The Bearded Seal (*Erignathus barbatus*) and Steller's Sea Lion (*Eumetopias jubatus*) also have long whiskers—the longest of Steller's Sea Lion are about 46 cm (1 ft 6 in) long.

Seals have quite an assortment of enemies. In

BELOW Neither the tiny eyes nor the bristly muzzle of this lumbering Amazon Manatee (*Trichechus inunguis*) are alluring, but these animals are reputedly responsible for the mermaid myth.

RIGHT A Sea Leopard or Leopard Seal (*Hydrurga leptonyx*) takes in air at the surface through its open nostrils. This specimen was captured in waters near Hawkes Bay, in New Zealand.

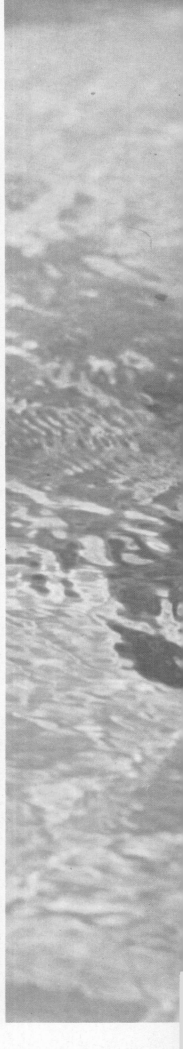

warm waters, sharks are probably their main predator and off the Galapagos, Tiger Sharks and the local Galapagos Shark, are known to take pups of both the Sea Lion and the Fur Seal. Killer Whales are ubiquitous killers of seals. In Arctic waters, Polar Bears (*Thalarctos maritimus*), kill many seals, while in Antarctica, Leopard Seals take pups of the other seals. Pups on land or ice may be attacked by a range of smaller predators; Arctic foxes dig Ringed Seal (*Pusa hispida*) pups out of their snow dens; bald Eagles attack Common Seal pups in Alaska and Giant Petrels will go for Southern Elephant Seal (*Mirounga leonina*) pups that are in poor condition. Perhaps the most night-marish predation of this sort, however, is the report of vampire bats feeding off sea lion pups in caves off the Chilean coast. In addition to all this, mass seal mortalities have been reported, the cause of which is not really known. In 1953, for example, thousands of Crabeater Seals were found dead on pack ice in the Antarctic, and the cause was tentatively put down to disease. In 1948, 21,600 dead Northern Fur Seal pups were counted along a 2.4 kilometre (1.5 mile) stretch of Alaska and their death was thought to have been caused by a bloom of toxic microscopic plants, known as a red tide. These plants are filtered out of the water by herbivorous plankton and shellfish, and the toxins passed up through the food chain, accumulating at each stage until they result in the death of the seals. The most horrifying fact of all, however, is that none of these natural enemies come anywhere near to matching man's devastation of many seal colonies. Just one example is that of South Georgia—largest of the sub-antarctic islands, which the sealers began to exploit, immediately after its discovery in 1775 by Captain Cook. First they killed the Fur Seals and then they turned their gruesome attention to the Elephant Seals. By 1900, the population of both were so low, that sealing was no longer economic.

LEFT A bull Southern Elephant Seal (*Mirounga leonina*) mates with a cow from his harem. Notice the giant disparity in size between the sexes. The male's proboscis is deflated and hangs over its mouth.

RIGHT The wide open gape adopted by a Southern Elephant Bull (*Mirounga leonina*) during its threat display, reveals the bright pink mouth lining. The nostrils open at the end of the proboscis.

Happily, in this case the ability of some animal populations to recover quickly was illustrated after the licensing system was introduced in 1910. Exploitation is still allowed, but is strictly controlled and although quotas allow the killing of about 6,000 seals a year, only large males over 3.2m (10ft 6in) may be taken. Each of these animals yields about 454 litres (100 gallons) of oil.

Largest of all the pinnipeds is the Southern Elephant Seal with the bulls averaging just over 5m (16ft 6in) and weighing about 2,200kg (4,818lb). The cows are about two thirds this length, and because they are more slimly built, weigh only about a fifth as much. The largest recorded bull Elephant Seal was killed at Possession Bay, South Georgia in 1913; it was 6.8m (22ft 6in) long and must have weighed about 4 tonnes. Elephant Seals occur all round the Antarctic, forming great breeding rookeries on most of the sub-antarctic islands that are close to the Antarctic Convergence—islands such as Kerguelen, Macquarie and South Georgia. The Antarctic Convergence is the name given to a circumpolar feature of the ocean currents which is a very important ecological boundary in the Antarctic Ocean. The incredible abundance of plankton in this ocean is related to the Convergence and the Elephant Seals feed on the massive concentration of squid and fish that occur there. They are reported as diving to depths of approximately 600m (768ft) in pursuit of their prey.

The bull Elephant Seals come ashore to the breeding rookeries during the Antarctic spring in early September and the cows begin to assemble the same month. Intense inter-bull rivalry occurs for possession of the female harems and fights start with posturing and roaring—so loud it can be heard for quite some distance. Each bull rears up and tries to overtop his rival while inflating his grotesque nose pouches. The encounter may end with the retreat of the challenger, or it may develop into a vicious battle with each bull inflicting heavy wounds on the other. The blood of seals clots in about five seconds—a great asset for such a violent life style.

The dominant bull will mate with the cows once they have weaned the pups, which are suckled for about twenty-three days. During this time the cows do not feed, and will each lose about 300kg (660lb) during suckling, while the pups grow at nearly 10kg (22lb) a day. As soon as the pups are weaned, the cows and bulls both return to the sea for a feast after their prolonged period of starvation. The pups stay in the rookery until their first moult, living off their blubber; then after a month of starvation they begin to feed on crustaceans and move out to sea. There is a high mortality rate

LEFT A Northern Sea Elephant bull (*Mirounga angustirostris*) threatens his rivals by rearing his head with its inflated proboscis. Female Sea Elephants do not have these inflatable pouches.

ABOVE Amongst these Crab-Eater Seals (*Lobodon carcinophagus*), hauled out on Antarctic pack ice, can be seen several scarred pelts. These are caused by territorial fighting between the males, and by attacks from Killer Whales.

among the pups, many of which die from a combination of the sun and their own body warmth thawing a pit beneath them, out of which they are unable to climb.

The Northern Elephant Seal (*Mirounga angustirostris*) breeds on the islands offshore California and Baia California. It is slightly smaller than the southern species and as the specific part of its scientific name suggests, its skull is narrower. Its proboscis is much longer and hangs down as much as 30 cm (1 ft) or more in front of its mouth. These seals feed mostly on various bottom-living animals such as skate, squid and rat-fish—the latter of which occur only at depths well in excess of 100 m (30 ft). On land, even during the breeding season, these huge seals are extremely placid, and there is little evidence of the vicious territorial fighting practised by their southern counterparts.

The Northern Elephant Seal is another species that has suffered devastation at the hands of man. In the early 19th century, enormous herds were found the length of California, but by 1880, exploitation had left only a single small herd. Even so, killing continued and in the next five years, a

further 294 were wiped out, at which time the species was thought to be extinct. Then, in 1907 a small herd was found on Guadalupe Island, West of Mexico and fourteen of the hundred animals were collected as museum specimens. Partial protection was given to the herd in 1911 and complete protection in 1922. The present estimated population of 10-15,000 Northern Elephant Seals have all descended from this one small herd.

In the Arctic, the Elephant Seal's counterpart is the Hooded Seal. These animals live in the eastern half of the North Atlantic from Newfoundland up round both sides of Greenland, around Iceland and as far north as Spitsbergen and Bear Island. They venture out into deep water, feeding on fish and squid in mid water, or bottom-living invertebrates such as starfish and sea urchins. However, comparatively little is known of their diet since they are usually collected during breeding, when they do not feed. Pups are born in late spring on ice floes, and are suckled for a fortnight, before being abandoned. The pups then moult, and a fortnight later, take to the sea. The males grow to a length of 3.5 m (11 ft 6 in) and weigh 400 kg (880 lb) while

the females are a little shorter than this and are appreciably lighter. The most remarkable characteristic of the male is its ability, when annoyed, to blow out a big scarlet bladder 15 cm (6 in) in diameter, from one nostril. Eskimos hunt these seals extensively as they prefer its meat to that of any other species. In addition each year about 50,000 Hooded Seals are taken by the Danes and Norwegians, of which just over half are pups. These are known as blue-backs and are exploited for their beautiful coats, as well as their oil and hide. In fact it is impossible to give exact figures

BELOW An adult male Hooded Seal (*Crystophora cristata*) inflates its nasal bladder or 'hood' with air, when it is threatened by another male or by approaching humans. The hood is fully inflated for 1-4 seconds.

of the numbers taken, as the sealers take both Hooded and Harp Seals together in the season, which is restricted to one month a year. The areas of exploitation are also restricted and only one cull is allowed a year in any one place.

The rarest seal in the world is the West Indian Monk Seal (*Monachus tropicalis*), which may already be extinct. These seals were the first mammals to be recorded by Columbus from the New World and their abundance was remarked on by early travellers and explorers like Dampier and Sir Hans Sloane. Off the Bahamas, fishermen would take as many as a hundred in one night, but since 1885, few have even been seen. The last certain record was of two sighted off Jamaica in 1949. The Hawaiian Monk Seal (*Monachus schauinslandi*), which occurs on the atolls of the Leeward Chain of islands to the north-west of Hawaii, almost suffered the same fate. The present population is probably still below 2,000, and despite conservation efforts, it is still suffering from human interference. This is the largest of the Monk Seals; the males reach a length of just over 2 m (7 ft) and weigh about 175 kg (385 lb); while the

ABOVE A newly born
Weddell Seal pup
(*Leptonychotes weddelli*)
with its fur still wet,
nuzzles up to its mother.
The pups are born with a
thick woolly natal coat.

RIGHT The threat posture
adopted by this Leopard
Seal (*Hydrurga leptonyx*),
shows this aggressive
predator's formidable
teeth. It feeds on fish,
penguins and young seals.

females are slightly longer and as much as 100 kg (220 lb) heavier. The third Monk Seal species is the Mediterranean Monk Seal (*Monachus monachus*) which occurs in scattered small groups throughout the Mediterranean, and on one or two Atlantic islands. Adults are nearly 3 m (9 ft) long. The Monk Seals are the only true seal species that live in warm tropical or sub-tropical seas, but their present rarity excludes the possibility of scientific study of their physiology, to see if they have any adaptations to life in warm seas.

There are four true seals that occur in the Southern Ocean, and of these, the Crabeater Seals, with a possible population of 5 million animals, are the most abundant pinniped in the world. The reason for their abundance is probably that they have never been used commercially because the hides are usually heavily scarred. The small scars on the males round the head and neck are believed to be caused by inter-seal fighting, while the long parallel gashes sometimes found, are thought to be the result of encounters with Killer Whales. Both sexes reach a length of about 3 m (10 ft) and mature after two to three years. They feed exclusively on krill—the food of baleen or whalebone whales—which they sieve out of the water by their complex teeth cusps. Crabeaters usually feed in the vicinity of the edge of the pack ice. They breed in thick pack ice in the Antarctic spring in areas which are totally inaccessible to man, so little is known of their breeding habits.

The most infamous seal in the Antarctic is the Leopard Seal, which is solitary but widespread, and occurs from the pack ice northwards to many of the Sub-Antarctic Islands. The 3.75 m (11 ft 6 in) females are unusual in being larger than the males

which are 3.25 m (10 ft). They are aggressive predators, feeding on fish, squid, penguins and pups of other seals. They have a particularly large and powerful head, and their rounded snout and large mouth, gives them a distinctly reptilian look. Their teeth have three long pointed cusps which are associated with the carnivorous diet of large animals, and they have an extraordinary, and rather macabre, ability to shake a penguin clean out of its skin and feathers. The Leopard Seal's reputation seems largely to be based on its evil appearance, allied to its inability to use its flippers on land; instead it crawls along with an obscene looping movement. There are no records of unprovoked attacks on man; but even so, divers in Antarctic waters treat them with utmost respect and wariness. The pups are born in November to December, but as breeding occurs within pack ice, nothing is known about the duration of suckling.

The sluggish Weddell Seals hardly ever move out of sight of the Antarctic mainland—a habitat which is far too inaccessible to have been invaded by man. In these cold seas they feed on squid, crustaceans and fish. They are tubby animals over 3 m (10 ft) long and they weigh about 400 kg (880 lb). They overwinter under the ice, biting through to keep their blow-holes open. After an initial fifty per cent mortality of the pups, Weddell Seals survive better after weaning than the Crabeaters, but their expectation of life is shorter, for as the teeth wear out they can no longer bite through the ice to keep their blow-holes open. Accounts from explorers tell of eerie sounds that waft up from the ice as the seals call to each other underneath. Pupping in Weddell Seals starts after the cows have assembled in rookeries in September to October

PRECEDING PAGE A female Weddell Seal (*Leptony-chotes weddelli*) and her pup surface in the Antarctic waters. The pup is suckled for six to seven weeks, before feeding on crustaceans.

RIGHT A young Walrus (*Odobenus rosmarus*), has not yet begun to grow its tusks, but it already has its stiff whiskers. At this stage, its skin is covered with a short coat of reddish hair.

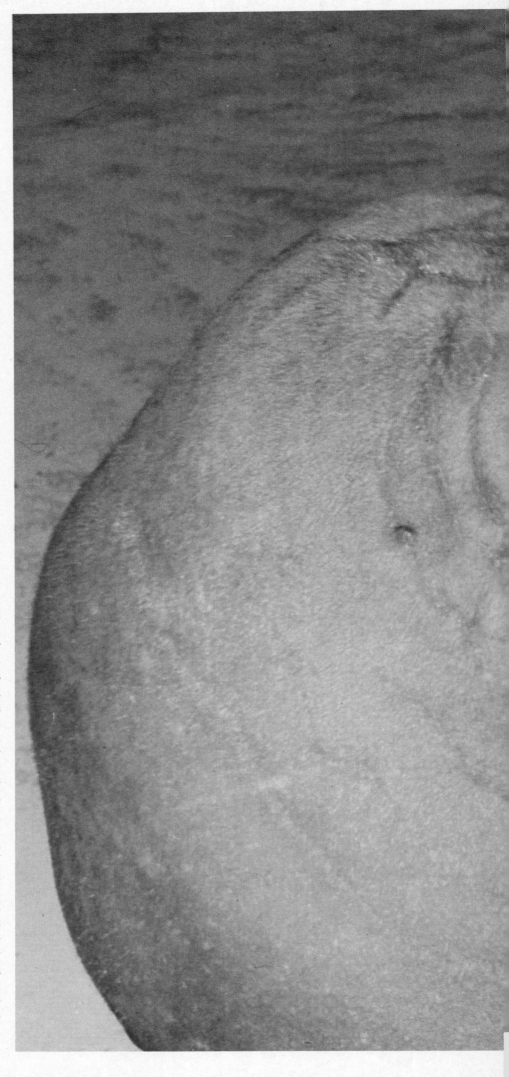

and the males arrive about a fortnight after pupping, to fight for possession of the females. Mating occurs when the pups are weaned, six weeks after birth.

The rarest of the Antarctic Seals is the Ross Seal (*Ommatophoca rossi*)—a solitary species which lives amongst the heaviest pack ice. It has a plump body, large flippers and a short and wide head. Its mouth is rather small but its eyes are enormous—probably because of the life it leads in the dimly lit waters beneath the ice. The seals may also use echo-location to find their food, which mostly consists of squid.

There are six further species of true seals found in northern seas, many of which are the most thoroughly studied of all pinnipeds. The Grey Seal is an inhabitant of rocky shores in the North Atlantic and has one population in the Gulf of St. Lawrence and Newfoundland, another off North-west Europe—centred on Scotland and a third in the Baltic. Little is known about the habits of this seal at sea, and similarly, because their digestion is so rapid, little is known of their diet, although, fishermen accuse them of damaging fisheries and nets. They are the proven carriers of a nematode—the codworm—which renders commercial fish unsaleable (although perfectly safe) for human consumption. The European population breeds in rookeries with the males guarding territories and mating occurs two weeks after pupping, although implantation of the fertilized eggs is delayed for three months until after the females have moulted. Grey seals have been aged by counting the layers of cement on the canine teeth, and ages confirmed by branding some animals. From this, it has been determined that the cows live up to thirty years, whereas the bulls rarely live longer than fifteen years. The cows start to breed at the end of their fifth year, while the bulls, on the other hand, are not able to hold a territory until their ninth or tenth year. The bulls are so exhausted and lose so much blubber in the six weeks they spend defending their territory, that their moult occurs several weeks later than the cows. Loss of blubber means loss of insulation, loss of food reserves and loss of buoyancy in the water. Survival of the bulls is better in the Canadian population, where the ratio of bulls to cows is one to one, and no territory is held. Instead there are isolated breeding pairs which haul out on ice. It is interesting, too, that the pups in the Canadian population also retain their first white woolly coat longer than the European animals. In general pups of species that are born on ice floes retain their juvenile white coats until the end of suckling; in species which breed on land, the juvenile coat is either brown, or white—in which case it is moulted prior to, or soon after, birth.

The Common or Harbour Seal is a good example of a species that habitually pups on sandbanks. It is very much an inshore or estuarine seal and it occurs widely in the Atlantic and Pacific north of 30°N. It appears to be unable to sleep in water, as most other seals can, which explains why it is more tied to the land. There are several isolated populations that show minor differences and are considered to be subspecies. Common seals feed mainly on bottom fishes found in shallow water, such as flounder, plaice, goby and dabs. These seals have long been exploited by man, as shown by the fact that their bones turn up in the kitchen middens of Bronze and Iron Age times. The Vikings hunted them and the Eskimos still hunt them for meat and raw hide, and today they are subjected to carefully controlled culls, to keep their populations down to a level where their damage to fisheries is not too serious.

The Bearded Seal occurs farther north and is an example of an inshore species which is found right round the Arctic Ocean. Its colloquial name is derived from its long whiskers, which are straight when the seals are in the water, but curl when they are dry. Although these seals are solitary animals, they are insatiably curious—a habit which can be fatal with hunters around. And the hunters certainly are around, for the Bearded Seals are extremely important to Eskimos for their hides, meat and blubber. In fact, the only part of the Bearded Seal meat which is not eaten is the liver and this is because it is so rich in vitamin A, that it is actually poisonous. The bulls of this species grow to nearly 4m (13ft) long and weigh about 450kg (992lb). These seals are thought to be able to dive to quite considerable depths to grub up worms, clams, shrimps, crabs and slow moving fishes from the sea bed. They do not form any sort of breeding rookeries and pupping occurs on ice floes. Mating occurs some time after the pups are born, but the females that have just produced pups do not ovulate until the males' sexual activity has ceased, so they pup only every second year. Even when females are successfully impregnated, implantation is delayed for about ten weeks. The pups tend to accompany their mothers for several months.

There are numerous subspecies of the Ringed Seal—a small species which occurs throughout the Arctic even at the North Pole and feeds in shallow water on small shrimps and fish. Both sexes are only about 1.4m (4ft) long and weigh about 90kg (200lb). In addition, there have been reports of a dwarf form which is only 60cm (2ft) long but some specialists are sceptical about its existence. Pups are born on land fast ice, in a lair under snow or in natural ice hollows which communicate with the water below the ice. Mating occurs while the cow is still suckling the calf, but implantation is delayed for over three months.

The Banded or Ribbon Seal (*Histriophoca fasciata*) is a rare species occurring in small herds on ice floes in the Sea of Okhotsk and Bering Sea. The Harp Seal (*Pagophilus groenlandicus*) lives in much the same environment in the North-west Atlantic, but it is very much more an animal of open water, and is much more abundant. It forms large breeding rookeries in amongst heavy pack ice and it is these rookeries that come under heavy exploitation. Two thirds of the annual cull of half a million Harp Seals are cubs—killed for their fur. Adults are killed for the oil from their blubber.

The well-known Walrus is found only in Northern waters. Instead of fur, it has a 5cm (2in) thick hide and this is underlain by about 6cm (2.5in) of blubber. The males grow to lengths of nearly 4m (13ft) and weigh about 1200kg (2645lb), while the females are slightly shorter and weigh about half as much. Both males and females have voracious appetites—as illustrated by a zoo specimen which used to eat 60kg (132lb) of fish a day—and they use their characteristic whiskers to locate their staple food of bottom-living clams. These, they reputedly stir out of the mud with their long tusks which they also use to help them clamber onto ice floes. The fact that the tusks are pure ivory has made them of great value to man and as a result, walruses have been hunted and indiscriminantly massacred with great enthusiasm. Another of their characteristic features are their extraordinary pharyngeal pouches which can be inflated to give sleeping walruses buoyancy in the water. They also act as a resonating chamber to produce a loud, ringing noise during courtship.

As well as the fur seals, the eared seals include in their group the sea lions, of which there are five species. The largest of all is Steller's Sea Lion and the huge heavily-maned males may weigh as much as 1000kg (2200lb). Steller's Sea Lion occurs in the North Pacific from the Sea of Okhotsk down to the northern parts of California, where it is replaced by the Californian Sea Lion, which extends down to Lower California. Isolated populations also occur off Japan and the Galapagos. The Japanese subspecies, which inhabits the south half of Honshu Island, is close to extinction. The Southern Sea Lion (*Otaria byronia*) occurs round the South American continent from Peru to the southern end of Brazil. The other two species—Australian Sea Lion (*Neophoca cinerea*) which inhabits the Great Australian Bight, and Hooker's Sea Lion (*Phocarctos hookeri*), from Auckland and the Campbell Islands—are not particularly abundant. Most sea lions feed on fish and squid, together with which, they also tend to swallow fairly large quantities of stones.

The eight species of fur seals comprise the most

valuable commercial seals. One species—the Northern Fur Seal—occurs in sufficient numbers to provide a good example of the efficacy of controlled cropping and conservation, in marked contrast to the disastrous uncontrolled cropping of the Guadalupe Fur Seal (*Arctocephalus philippi*). Most of the Northern Fur Seals live on the Pribilof Islands, north of the Aleutians in the Bering Sea. When these islands were discovered in 1786, sealing began at once, and 2.5 million seal skins were taken by the Russians in the next eighty years. When the USA bought Alaska in 1870 an annual quota of 100,000 was imposed and, legally, only males could be taken. However, animals were killed in the water where they could not be sexed accurately and many sank before their bodies could be recovered. Poaching was rife and the population was drastically reduced until sealing

ABOVE A New Zealand Fur Seal (*Arctocephalus forsteri*) amongst a *Macrocystis* kelp bed on the Kiakoura coast in the South Island, displays aggressively towards the photographer.

LEFT AND RIGHT Galapagos Fur Seals (*Arctocephalus australis galapagoensis*) were once heavily exploited by fur traders. They are seen here in the act of submerging (left) and idling offshore Geonovesa Island (right).

LEFT A Dugong (*Dugong dugon*) escorted by fish in shallow tropical sea water. It swims using its pair of flippers at the front and its flattened tail. It has no hind limbs.

BELOW A Manatee or Sea Cow (*Trichechus* spp.) rolls over beneath the surface showing how its forelimbs are used mainly for steering. Propulsion comes from beating the tail.

in the water was banned altogether. Now over 1.5 million live on the Pribilofs alone. The Northern Fur Seal is notable for its seasonal migration of about 10,000 kilometres (6,250 miles) which it travels round the North Pacific.

The Guadalupe Fur Seal exists in two widely separated locations—Guadalupe Island off west Mexico and Juan Fernandez off Chile. At the beginning of the 19th century, 3 million of these seals were killed off the Chilean islands alone, and in fact, both populations were thought to be extinct by 1880. In 1926 a small group was found on Guadalupe and two males were collected and taken to the San Diego Zoo. Unfortunately the man who discovered the herd quarrelled with the Zoo's Director and he returned to the Island to kill the rest of the herd. He took the skins to Panama to sell them where he was killed in a bar-room brawl. Another colony was found in 1954 on Guadalupe and recently another on Juan Fernandez.

The Kerguelen Fur Seal (*Arctocephalus tropicalis*) was another species to be almost exterminated by sealers. A small colony of these krill-eating seals was rediscovered in 1933 at Bird Island off South Georgia. Under the complete protection now afforded them this colony has grown at an incredible rate and is currently producing about 60,000 cubs a year. It is estimated that the population may soon top the two million mark.

The Sea Cows or sirenians are reputed to have given rise to the mermaid myth, although it is sometimes hard to see why, for their physical ugliness is virtually unsurpassed throughout the animal kingdom! The largest species—Steller's Sea Cow (*Hydrodamalis stelleri*)—was the largest vegetarian marine mammal to have lived in cold waters, and amazingly, these 4-5000 kg (8180-11000 lb) beasts sustained their great bulk on seaweed. Within twenty-seven years of their discovery in Alaska, they were exterminated. A relative of Steller's Sea Cow, the Dugong (*Dugong dugon*), is found in the shallow tropical seas around the Indian Ocean, although the only large populations now surviving, occur along the south of New Guinea and along the Queensland coast in Australia. Slow, placid, solid-boned animals, very little is known about their life style, behaviour and habits. They look somewhat like porpoises with a pair of flippers as fore-limbs, and their flattened muzzle has mobile fleshy side lobes, which carry short bristles. They have no hind limbs and their tail is expanded into a horizontal fluke. Eel and turtle grasses form their staple diet, and they are hunted for their fat and oil, which is used medicinally, and their meat, which is good eating and is reputed to have aphrodisiac properties.

The other species of Sea Cow, the Manatees (*Trichechus* spp) are mostly riverine animals although they do venture out into estuarine areas. One of the largest concentrations of these quaint animals occurs in the estuary of the Miami River, in the centre of the city. They are gregarious beasts, and will gather into herds, dispersing at night to feed. In the sea they eat only eel grasses.

Squids, Octopuses and Clams

By no means all inhabitants of the deep are vertebrate animals. Squids, octopuses and clams are all marine molluscs which can certainly claim such a title and they tend to evoke feelings of fear and horror in man. Related to terrestrial slugs and snails, squids, cuttlefish and octopuses are cephalopod molluscs which are confined to the sea. The giant squids (*Architeuthis* spp.), are the heaviest invertebrate animals, in the world, but since relatively few intact specimens have been caught, both the maximum weight and length attained by these animals is somewhat speculative. To add to the speculation even further, their tentacles are highly elastic.

The largest, and certainly the heaviest specimen so far discovered, was an *Architeuthis princeps* found stranded on 2 November 1878 in Canada, at Thimble Tickle Bay, Newfoundland. Its overall length was 14 m (55 ft), of which 6 m (20 ft) was its body and head and 11m (35 ft), its tentacles. Two fishermen spotted the giant squid which had become grounded, from their boat, and as the tide ebbed down the shore, they could see more and more of the huge monster. The fishermen threw a grapnel at it and then tied the end of the rope to a tree on the shore, keeping a safe distance, until the enormous arms stopped writhing. After the squid—which, with an estimated weight of 2 tonnes, was the largest ever captured—had died, it was cut up for dog meat.

A few years later, in 1887, a 16.5 m (57 ft) long giant squid (*Architeuthis longimanus*) was washed ashore in Lyall Bay, New Zealand. Although this was longer than the specimen found off Newfoundland, it doesn't rate the title of the 'largest' as the greater proportion of its length was its extensive 15 m (49 ft) long tentacles. The longevity of these giant squids is unknown.

Squids generally have a torpedo-shaped body with small side fins at one end, which are used for slow speed swimming. They can achieve rapid movements by their jet propulsive mechanism, operated by water being violently squirted out from the mantle—a highly muscular bag—through a siphon that can be pointed forwards, sideways or backwards. The fins of giant squids are particularly small in proportion to their overall body size, and these, together with other anatomical features, suggest that, unless they are provoked, giant squids are slow swimmers.

Extending from a squid's head end are eight suckered arms and a pair of longer, extensible tentacles. These contract down towards the suckered arms, and are used to catch the squid's prey, which it then tears at with its hard, central beak. Hooked like a parrot's, the beak is extremely tough, but unlike a parrot, the lower mandible is longer and so overlaps the upper. Even small squids, less than 45 kg (100 lb) in weight, have been known to sever steel wires with their beaks. Amongst the invertebrates, cephalopod eyes are highly evolved, and play an essential part in hunting down the prey. Quite what the squid's prey is, however, is somewhat uncertain for digestion in these animals is very rapid.

Although rarely seen alive by man, the multi-armed giant squids have given rise to numerous myths and legends, including those of the Norwegian krakens, mentioned in Chapter 4. This name is derived from the Norwegian *krake*, meaning an enormous mythical sea monster reported to have been sighted off the Norwegian coasts. More than once, kraken have been credited with the ability to sink ships. Olaus Magnus referred to them in 1555 as, 'Monstrous fish . . one of these sea-monsters . . will drown easily many great ships . .

It was stories such as these, that inspired Jules Verne to relate his encounter between the submarine *Nautilus* and a giant kraken in his book *Twenty Thousand Leagues Under the Sea*. A 2 tonne rubber kraken was used in Walt Disney's film version of this book, and the arms of this monster were operated by twenty four men using electronic, hydraulic and compressed air systems.

Several centuries after Olaus Magnus's descriptions, Pierre Denys de Montfort, who worked in the Museum of Natural History in Paris, wrote six volumes entitled *Histoire Naturelle générale et particulière des Mollusques* which were published during the period 1802-5. He included a description of an imaginary *Poulpe colossal* (poulpe is French for octopus) which he stated was capable, along with others of its kind, of dragging several men-o'-war down into the depths. Since at that time, no-one had succeeded in capturing an intact giant squid, scientists did not believe this story, and it was not until half a century later that a scientist was at last able to measure, and thence describe the body of a giant squid.

During the 1870's, more giant squids came to light than during any decade since. Most of these

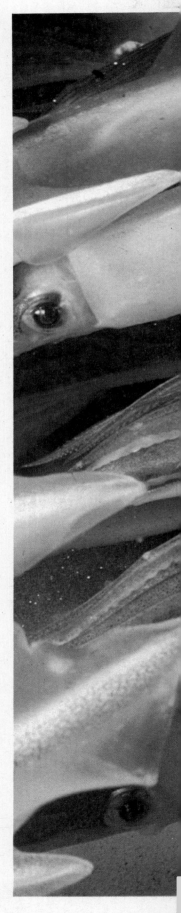

BELOW LEFT A large
octopus demonstrates the
characteristic features of
suckered arms (webbed in
this species), and small
globular body. Water
intake for the respiratory
current is below the eye.

BELOW Like many marine
animals, squid form dense
shoals when mating.
Their whole body shape
is designed for mid-water
swimming, whereas most
octopuses are bottom
living animals.

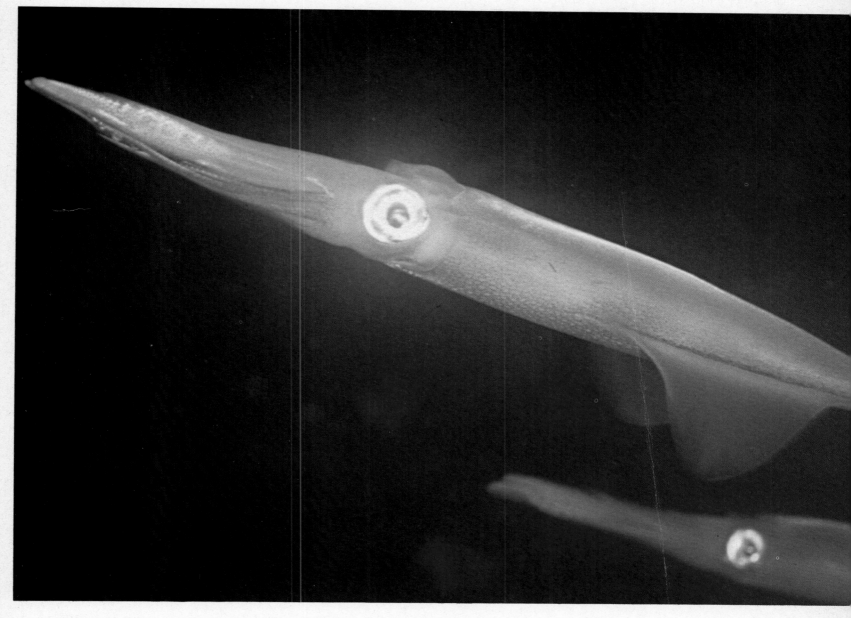

ABOVE Common squid (*Loligo vulgaris*) demonstrate the smoothness of their streamlined bodies. As well as their method of jet propulsion, they can use their fins for swimming.

LEFT Cuttlefish (*Sepia* sp.) are close relatives of octopus and squid. They are experts at colour change, and have curious shaped irises to their eyes.

were obtained off the Newfoundland coast, which like Norway, has an indented fjord coastline. In 1873, two squid encounters took place in New-foundland. The first was on 26 October, when two fishermen, plus one son, who was twelve years old, rowed over to an object they saw in the water. It turned out to be a giant squid which straight away struck the boat with its beak, wrapped a tentacle and an arm around it, and then began to drag it, fishermen and boy included, below the surface. It was lucky the fishermen had taken the boy along, for it was he who had the presence of mind to grab a tomahawk and sever the squid's enslaving arm and tentacle. As the squid disappeared down into the depths, they rapidly rowed ashore, where they threw the arm of the squid on to the beach to be eaten by dogs. The 5.8m (19ft) long portion of the tentacle was eventually taken to a naturalist, the Rev. Moses Harvey, who knew at once that it belonged to the mythical devil-fish, which no-one had succeeded in capturing. However he still needed the complete body for a proper description of the animal. He was to get it a few weeks later, when fishermen hauled a giant squid inside their herring net. One of the men managed to plunge his knife between the eyes and then to decapitate the squid. Harvey paid 10 dollars to have this specimen delivered to his house, where he preserved it in a

brine solution. Although it was small in compari-son to later captures—a mere 10m (32ft) long—it was the first complete specimen.

It is hard to believe that giant squids could succumb to any predator, but sucker marks on the head of Cachalots or Sperm Whales, and squid remains in their stomachs, as discussed earlier, are certain proof of these encounters. Indeed, the stomach contents of Sperm Whales provide scientists with the best source of giant squid re-mains—especially the beaks, which are undigested. As a Sperm Whale dies, it often vomits its stomach contents, which may include freshly caught squid.

The octopus is another animal that frequently features as a terrifying monster in novels and fiction films. Victor Hugo described a fight to the death between a man and an octopus in his story 'The Toilers of the Sea'. The facts, however, are less gruesome, and few octopuses grow to a size at which they are a real danger to man. The largest known species is the Common Pacific Octopus (*Octopus apollyon*), the record size for which is held by a specimen that was trapped in a fisher-man's net in Monterey Bay, California. It measured 6m (20ft) across its arms and weighed 50kg (110lb). Skin divers off the West Coast of the United States indulge in the dangerous sport of killing these big animals and unsubstantiated

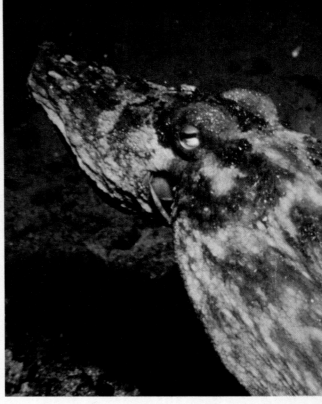

ABOVE AND RIGHT An octopus (*Octopus maorum*) is seen here, mating (above) with a female snug in her hideout, and (right) swimming by jet propulsion.

BELOW Stranded by the ebbing tide, a curled octopus (*Eledone cirrhosa*) crawls across the sand trying to find its way back to the water, before it becomes dried out.

FAR RIGHT The common Pacific octopus (*Octopus apollyon*) is the largest known species of octopus. It is quite capable of securely holding a diver underwater.

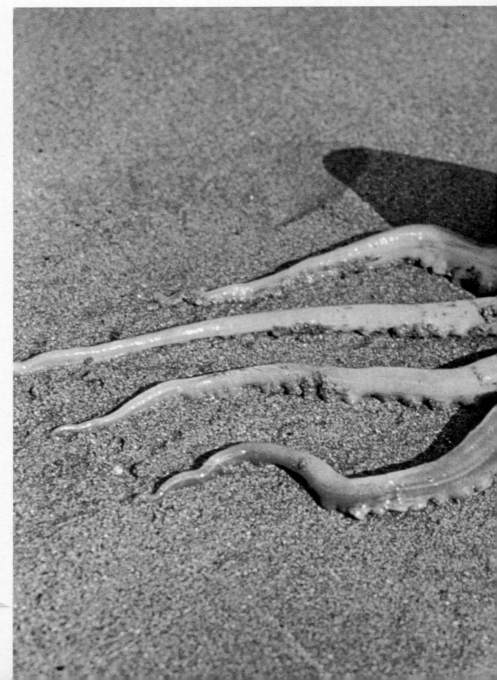

claims have been made for captures of animals up to 16.3m (28ft) across their arms.

The main danger an octopus presents to man, is that of holding him under the surface until he drowns, for once the suckers on its arms have taken hold of an object, their grip can be broken only by either ripping the sucker, or the surface off the object. A large octopus firmly holding on to a diver's arms or legs and anchoring itself to a rock is almost impossible to dislodge unless it can either be persuaded in some way to let go, or the diver can sever the octopus's arms.

An octopus can be killed by stabbing it between the eyes, where the brain lies just below the surface. Natives of the Gilbert Islands used to kill octopuses by biting into the brain in this vulnerable spot. The natives worked in pairs. One of them, acting as the human bait, would swim down to the lair of the octopus, covering his eyes with one hand so as to protect them from the treacherous tentacles. Once the octopus had embraced him, his mate dived down and bit the octopus between the eyes. Split second timing was obviously very crucial! If a lone diver is investigated by a large octopus, the best policy is to remain motionless; an octopus will soon lose interest in an apparently lifeless object.

The octopus has a larger brain for its size than any other animal without a backbone and experiments have shown that its intelligence matches the size of its brain. The Mediterranean octopus builds itself a little home of stones on the ocean bottom, and there it spends the day, emerging at night to hunt for its food of crabs. It has been shown to be able to recognize shapes, and to respond to changes in the layout of its territory. Its eyes are very similar in design to our own, and an octopus's vision is probably as good as ours. In one respect the octopus's eye is superior, for whereas the nerves in the human eye pass over the inner

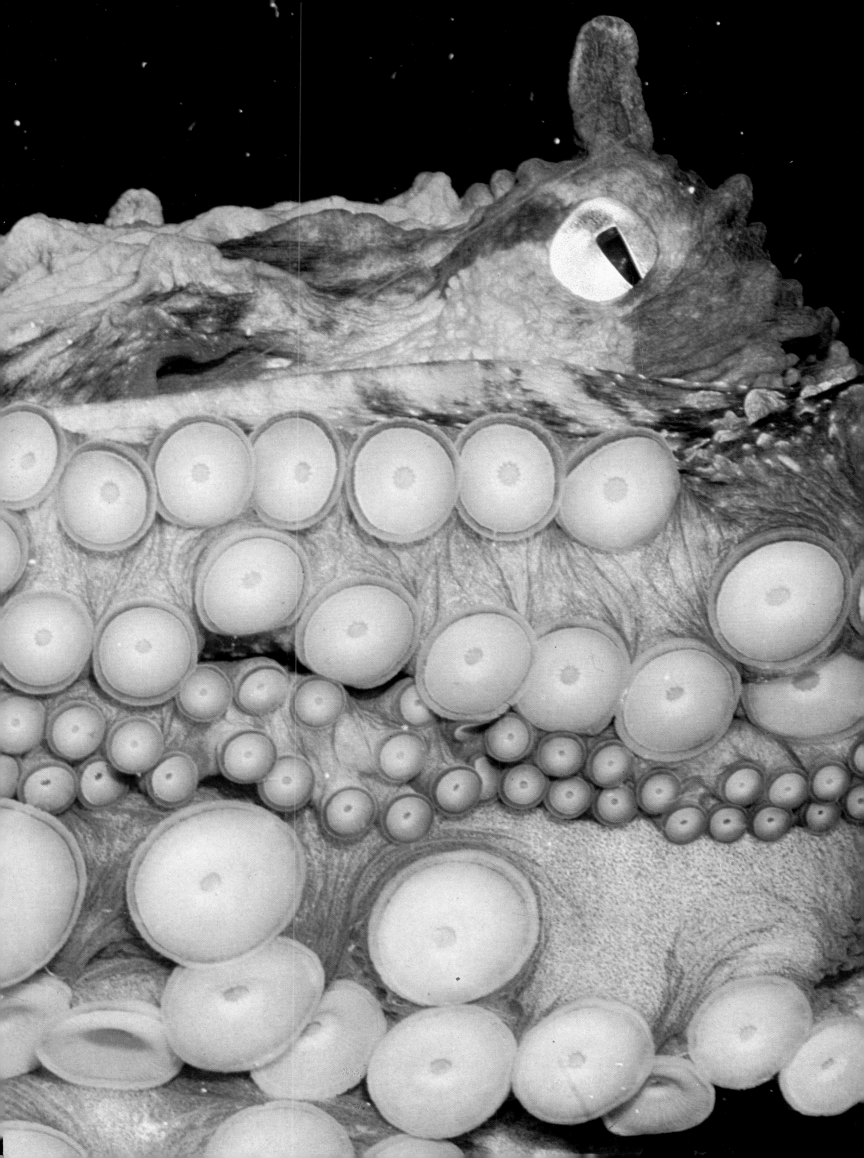

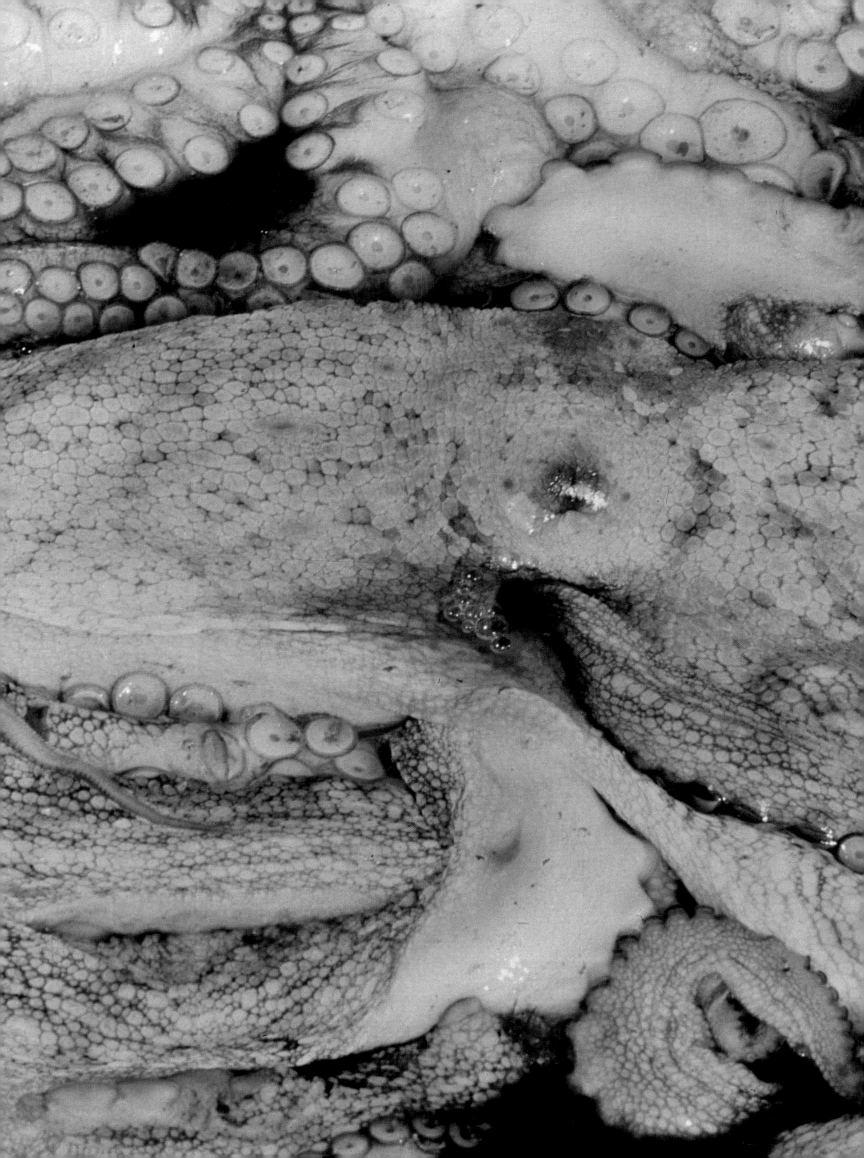

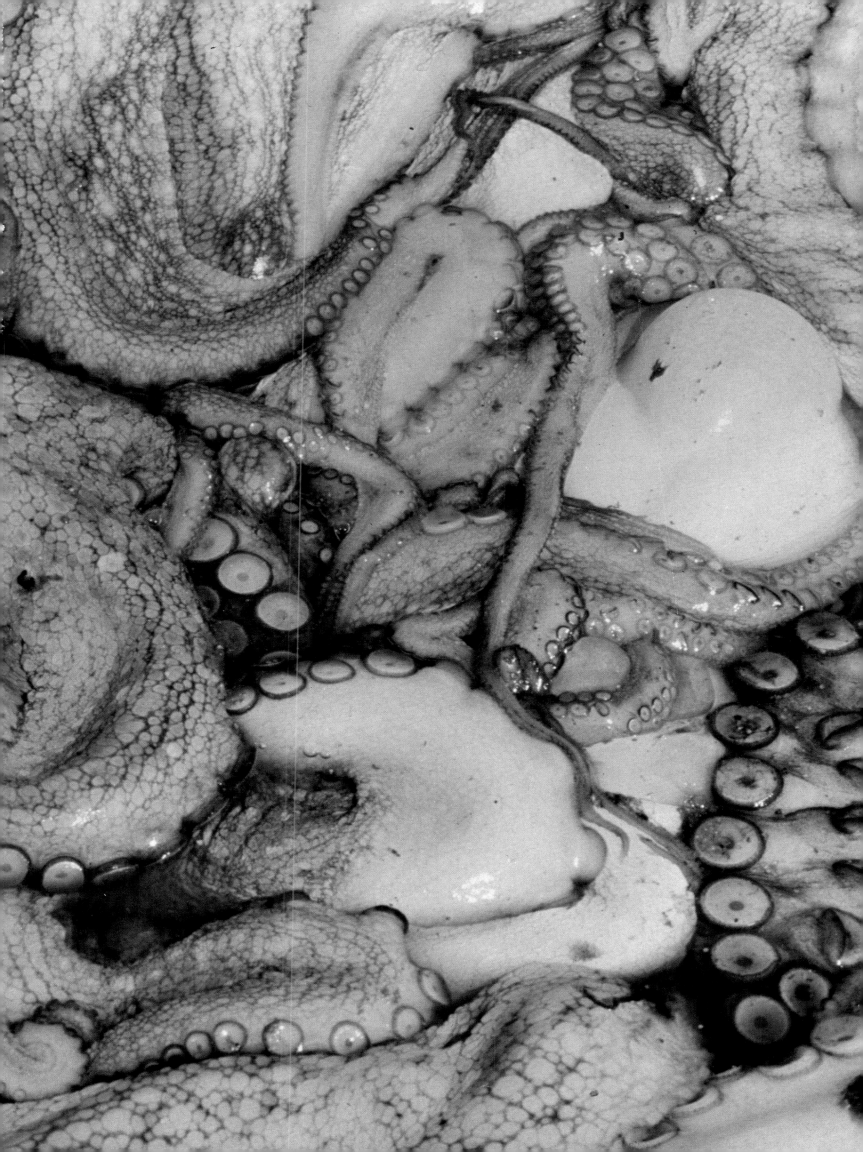

LEFT This close-up of the mantle of a giant clam (*Tridacna gigas*), found off Mauritius, shows the row of eye-spots along the edge of the mantle and the siphon, just emerging from between the valves.

RIGHT The blue mantle folds of a tropical reef clam (*Tridacna* sp.) are studded with simple eyes. If a shadow falls across the eyes, the clam snaps the valves of its shell tightly shut.

BELOW Peering between the upper two of its eight suckered arms is the eye of this common octopus (*Octopus vulgaris*). An octopus's vision is probably as good as man's, and optically its eye is better designed.

They are exposed by the gape of the shell and are vivid colours of blue, green or purple, studded with single eyes which respond to shadows passing over the clam. The clam snaps shut its two massive valves to protect its soft internal tissues, with a thick single adductor muscle, which draws the valves together with impressive strength. The danger presented by this animal to divers, is that if they are pre-occupied by a task or some other hazard, they may inadvertently step between the valves of a giant clam. They will shut like an old fashioned man-trap. Hans Haas demonstrated the efficiency of these valves on cine film, using artificial legs. They were convincingly crushed! The possible saving grace, however, is that the valves do not close very rapidly.

The giant clams are one of many animals which form the tropical coral reefs and when the tide recedes, they gape open their valves, spreading out their mantle folds. Within the mantle, live symbiotic microscopic algae called zooxanthellae, which require sunlight to photosynthesize and thereby to grow and reproduce. The giant clams 'farm' these algae within their mantle folds, and use them as a secondary source of food; the additional nourishment may account for giant clams far exceeding the size of any other bivalve mollusc.

The largest natural pearl formation was found inside a giant clam (*Tridacna derasa*) in the Philippine Islands in May 1934. This irregularly shaped opaque pearly mass measured 24.8 cm (9.5 in) long and weighed 127,374 grains (18 lb 5 oz), a vast size when compared with the largest pearl in the world which weighed a mere 1,800 grains (4 oz).

Index